OUTHERN LITERATURE IN TRANSITION

SOUTHERN LITERATURE IN TRANSITION

HERITAGE AND PROMISE

edited by

Philip Castille and William Osborne

MEMPHIS STATE UNIVERSITY PRESS

Manufactured in the United States of America

International Standard Book Number 0-87870-209-1

Contents

Preface

Writing in 1933, William Faulkner undertook to examine the relation of art and region in America. In his self-conscious estimation, the prospects for the southern writer were dim compared to opportunities in the East and Midwest. Art in New York "is part of the glitter or shabbiness of the streets," he pronounced. In Chicago, it is "lusty, loudvoiced, always changing and always young." The rapid rhythms of these northern cities seemed to suggest immense life and teeming artistic possibilities.

By contrast, the South as a place offered little, if anything, to sustain its writers. In Faulkner's judgment, authentic southern culture had ended in 1865. What had replaced it was an ersatz product,

> a thing known whimsically as the New South. . . . a land of Immigrants who are rebuilding the towns and cities into replicas of towns and cities in Kansas and Iowa and Illinois, with skyscrapers and striped canvas awnings instead of wooden balconies, and teaching the young men who sell the gasoline and waitresses in the restaurants to say O yeah? and to speak with hard r's, and hanging over the intersections of quiet and shaded streets where no one save Northern tourists in Cadillacs and Lincolns ever pass at a gait faster than a horse trots, changing red-and-green lights and savage and peremptory bells.

Since this fraudulent and ugly land had no original life of its own, how could southern artists draw any vitality from it? In Faulkner's conclusion, they could not. They could only retreat within themselves, either "to draw a savage indictment of the contemporary scene or to escape from it into a makebelieve region of swords and magnolias and mockingbirds which perhaps never existed anywhere."

This extreme position, brimming with hostility and frustration, is deliberately polemical, and its adversary terms have been echoed and at times amplified by a half-century of southern writers since Faulkner. Nor was Faulkner the first southern writer to probe the anguished intersections of southern art and life. The antecedents of this ambivalence about southern cultural expression, about its quality and even its possibility, and about the self-worth of its often alienated and sometimes obsessive artists, long precede Faulkner's remarks. These tensions have engaged the southern mind since well before the Civil War, perhaps as far back as William Byrd II and Ebenezer Cook.

Do such heated questions as those Faulkner raises about southern literature and culture remain valid today? Were they ever, in fact, anything more than self-conscious posturings? If there is a literary heritage that deserves definition as "southern," does it yet hold promise for a literature recognizably regional? Does there even persist in the 1980s a sectional awareness on the part of southern writers? Have we exchanged New Souths for Old, and Newer Souths for these? Who are the "authentic" southern voices, which perhaps may be, in the dispersion of time, more resonant now than before? What do they tell us about their complex milieu, loving it or hating it, living it or leaving it? Can their documents and destinies really be considered special after all? Or, are matters of southerness only parochial at best, subsumed under greater headings of history and society, class and race, sex and selfhood?

These are complex questions. During the symposium, "Southern Culture in Transition: Heritage and Promise," held at Memphis State University on April 24–26, 1980, they were raised again and again. No one, of course, expected final answers. But in our view, valuable notes were provided through the spirited debates and discussions that followed the reading of papers by invited participants.

Our participants, it should be noted, were furnished in advance with such questions as those posed above, and all were encouraged to reconsider their own attitudes as well as popular stereotypes of southern literary criticism as they prepared their papers for presentation and defense at the symposium. As expected, the papers were varied in content and approach, half of them dealing with broad issues of southern writing and culture, and the other half focusing on specific writers and works. To reflect this difference in approach, we have divided the collection into two parts. But, finally, all essays are concerned with the same questions: "Have southern writers been affected by their regional roots?" and "If so, how or to what extent?"

The "answers" to these hypothetical questions, as one might expect, are multifarious and complex. To preserve something of the forensic character of the papers, we begin Part I with Cleanth Brooks (Yale University, Emeritus) whose essay takes an affirmative stand on the connection between southern writers and their milieu. Brooks fears that the links between writers and region will weaken as the South becomes less "southern" and more like the rest of the country. Two essayists who follow perceive region as less than vital. Elizabeth Hardwick (novelist and critic) argues that conditions for writing are accidental and unpredictable, and Noel Polk (University of Southern Mississippi) maintains that intellect and talent are more important than locale. Thomas L. McHaney (Georgia State University) examines the so-called Southern Renascence in light of the achievements of the international Modern Movement. And Lewis P. Simpson (Louisiana State University) suggests that the southern writer's sensibility is closer to the literary consciousness of Europe than to that of the American West.

Part II focuses on specific southern authors, their often ambiguous attitudes toward home, and their resistance to conventional patterns. Michael Millgate (University of Toronto) probes William Faulkner's ambivalent responses toward his region and the resulting tensions in his art. William Osborne (Memphis State University) finds similar dichotomies and contradictions in the thought and work of John Crowe Ransom, both critics asserting that Faulkner's and Ransom's work profited from this clash of views. Philip Castille (University of Houston, Downtown College) sees William Alexander Percy's autobiography as an ideological defense of planter-dominated southern hierarchic culture and an attack upon modern mass society. The section concludes with three critics showing how both male and female southerners faced literary and societal pressures. Michael Kreyling (Tulane University) explores the extent to which New Orleans writers Lafcadio Hearn, Grace King, and George Washington Cable felt pressured to write formulaic local color fiction. Miriam J. Shillingsburg (Mississippi State University) finds that Caroline Lee Hentz, Grace King, and Kate Chopin refused to conform to the stereotype of the Southern Woman Writer. And Thomas

Bonner, Jr. (Xavier University of Louisiana) affirms that Kate Chopin selected regional topics in her fiction to point up universal issues of self and society.

These generalizations are meant to be suggestive rather than definitive of the essays in this collection, and we invite the reader to make connections that we scarcely do more than hint at here. An essay not yet mentioned helped to suggest the grouping we employ. The late Professor C. Hugh Holman (University of North Carolina), whose paper was not presented at the symposium because of his illness, became the logical critic to lead off the collection. In his paper Professor Holman urged a fresh look at southern literature, free from cliché and category, and a new appreciation of the variety and vitality of the field. Happily, our participants appear to have thought along virtually identical lines, thereby making it possible for us to begin this volume with Professor Holman's challenge, to follow the challenge with our participants' responses, and finally to honor posthumously this remarkable champion of southern letters by highlighting what was probably his last major essay.

To conclude, all essays, including titles, have been revised for publication, and the essays on Ransom and Percy, while not read at the symposium, were included to round out the offerings. Funds for the symposium were provided by the Memphis State University President's Academic Enrichment Fund, the River City Writers Series, and the University Program Committee. Conference sponsors were the Department of English, the College of Arts and Sciences, and the Office of Continuing Education. The symposium was directed by Philip Castille, Members of the Symposium Committee were Roger R. Easson, H. Ramsey Fowler, William Osborne, Gordon Osing, and Louis Charles Stagg.

Editorial assistance was given by Joseph K. Davis, Chairman, Department of English, Walter R. Smith, and J. Lasley Dameron, Department of English, and J. Ralph Randolph, Director, Memphis State University Press.

Philip Castille
William Osborne

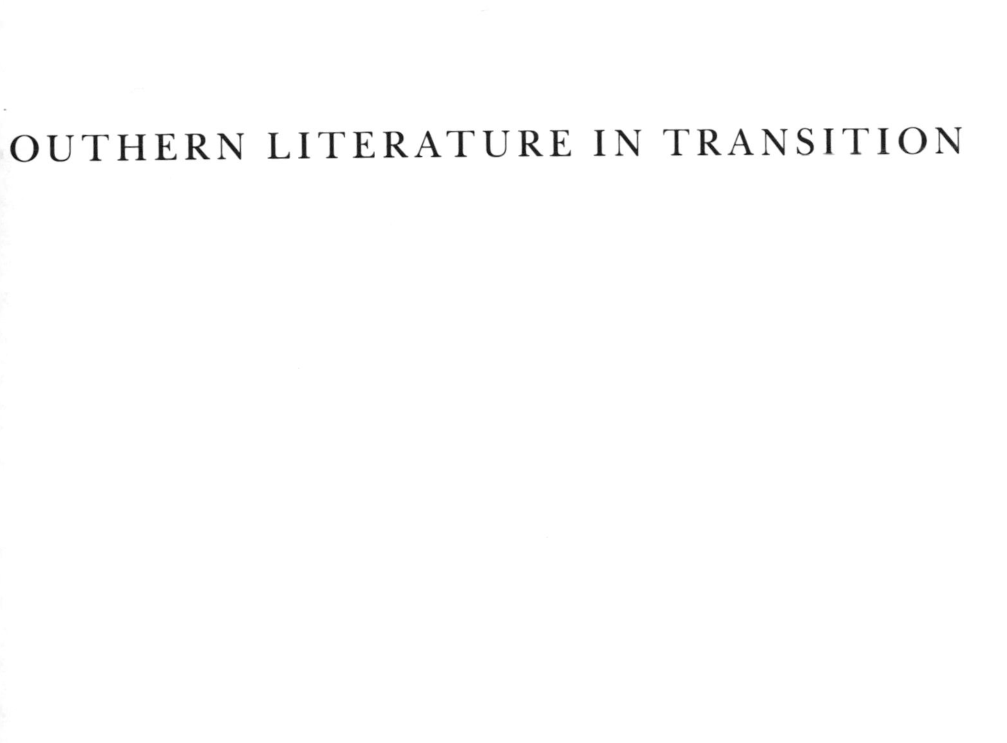

OUTHERN LITERATURE IN TRANSITION

C. Hugh Holman

No More Monoliths, Please: Continuities in the Multi-Souths

After more than thirty-five years of trying to understand things southern, I begin to think there are some things we should not be doing. In 1910, when he was approaching seventy and when, according to one of his biographers, he was "close to despair," Henry Adams addressed to his colleagues *A Letter to American Teachers of History*, attempting to show "possible ways of fighting the forces which were causing the despair."[1] I hasten to assure you that I am not in despair, but Adams wrote that *Letter*, as he wrote most things, out of his profound sense of failure. I, like Adams at least in the sense of failure, feel constrained, after all these years, to address to you A Letter to Teachers of Southern American Literature. My subject is small beside Adams' massive theory of entropy in history, although, of course, not so small as I am in comparison with the author of *Mont-Saint-Michel and Chartres*. But I am justified to some degree by the fact that whatever I say must be prefaced by my saying, "Mea culpa." The sins I shall attempt to point out are sins I know well, for I have been chief among their sinners. Let us, therefore, go to confession together, not with Adams' despair but with at least a modicum of hope.

We all suffer from a common human tendency to seek the controlling unity, the essential principle, the shaping archetype in everything we study. In a profoundly pluralistic world, we want to lay hands on the simple key. Richard Chase finds the romance to be the only valid form of American fiction. R. W. B. Lewis sees the archetypal American as a primitive innocent. R. P. Blackmur finds all American novels to be in the allegorical mode. William Spengemann sees travel-writing at the heart of the American literary experience. And such examples could be multiplied many times. Despite the southerner's vaunted admiration for the concrete, we who study southern writing have not proved immune to the disease. We too seek easy or inclusive answers. In the field of literary study the old monition, "Seek and ye shall find," is painfully true. Most of us, by omitting a little that cannot be made to fit, selecting from the rest rather carefully, and, like Procrustes, fitting what we select to our particular narrow beds, arrive at conveniently simple answers to the question of what southern literature is all about. The result is usually a schema in which a sentimentalized version of Scott was used defensively in the antebellum period, an exploitative local colorism dominated the postbellum period, and a glorious, even sacramental, agrarianism illumines the twentieth century.

May I illustrate by quoting an effusion from a piece written in my literary nonage, which attempts to summarize the characteristics of southern writing. It says:

> These characteristics are: a sense of evil, a pessimism about man's potential, a tragic sense of life, a deep-rooted sense of the interplay of past and present, a peculiar sensitivity to time as a complex element in narrative art, a sense of place as a dramatic dimension, and a thoroughgoing belief in the intrinsic value of art as an end in itself.[2]

Several people have done me the questionable honor of quoting that list approvingly, and I always feel a sense of discomfort when I see it quoted. What I was doing there, in my eagerness to find *the* tradition, seems to me very much like what many critics and historians of southern writing—particularly that of the so-called Southern Renascence—do in this search for unifying principles; and it is like what we condemn Thomas Nelson Page for doing in his extravagant praise of the past in *The Old South*.

I am led to these remarks by several recent books, among them Richard Gray's *The Literature of Memory*, Michael O'Brien's *The Idea of the American South*, and J. V. Ridgely's *Nineteenth Century Southern*

Literature. Without wishing to indict any of them, I would say that, despite many sophisticated merits, they share the simplistic fault of too limited a view of what southern writing has been and is. This fault has been made glaringly obvious by the publication of Richard Beale Davis's monumental *Intellectual Life in the Colonial South,* which meticulously avoids the error.

May I cite an example of what I mean? In his chapter "The Southern Romance: The Matter of Virginia"[3] Ridgely discusses John Davis's *The First Settlers of Virginia: Tales of an American Landlord,* George Tucker's *The Valley of Shenandoah,* and William A. Caruthers's *The Cavaliers of Virginia.* Following, with reservations, the strictures of Mark Twain and Rollin G. Osterweis, Ridgely sees these novels as clumsy and inaccurate imitations of Sir Walter Scott. Now certainly the influence of the Waverley novels is present, but more obviously present is the moralistic hero-portraiture of Jane Porter's *Scottish Chiefs,* at whose doorstep may be laid many of what we regard as the faults of Caruthers and the other early Virginia novelists. Also, before we decide to saddle Caruthers with the charge of being a knee-jerk Virginia aristocrat, it may be well to remember that he departed radically from the received standard Virginia view of slavery, being himself an abolitionist.

What I am trying to say is that the clichés about southern writing, however skillfully presented, leave out aspects which we ignore at the peril of misunderstanding our subject matter. In this respect I am reminded of a comment that U. B. Phillips made:

> The diversity shown [in my pictures of plantation life] may be surprising, but it would be surely be greater if more cases were available. Neither planters nor slaves, nor overseers . . . were cast in one mold—traditions, romances, diatribes and imaginative histories to the contrary not withstanding. Plantation life and industry had in the last analysis as many facets as there were periods, places, and persons involved. The régime nevertheless had a unity palpable always.[4]

Southern writing, like the plantation life that Phillips describes, certainly shared a number of distinctively regional characteristics, but its variety and diversity are even more important. And when we concentrate on the similarities, we run the risk of stripping from it much of its vitality. That wise lady Gertrude Stein expressed what I am trying to say very well:

> . . . the creator of the new composition in the arts is an outlaw until he is a classic. . . . For a very long time everybody refuses and then almost without a pause almost everybody accepts. . . . When the acceptance comes, by that acceptance the thing created becomes a classic. . . . The characteristic quality of a classic is that it is beautiful. Now of course it is perfectly true that a more or less first rate work of art is beautiful but the trouble is that when that first rate work of art becomes a classic because it is accepted the only thing that is important from then on to the majority of the acceptors the enormous majority, the most intelligent majority of the acceptors is that it is so wonderfully beautiful. Of course it is wonderfully beautiful, only when it is still a thing irritating annoying stimulating then all quality of beauty is denied to it.[5]

Does not that sound as though Gertrude Stein had foreseen the course of William Faulkner's reputation? Are we not in serious danger of making classically beautiful what in Faulkner was "irritating annoying stimulating" and constituted his special worth?

I think William Gilmore Simms can be used to illustrate my point. J. V. Ridgely, in *William Gilmore Simms,* concentrates his attention on the novels in the Redfield edition and sees him as the creator of an epic myth of the plantation aristocracy. Donald Davidson, in his Introduction to *The Letters of William Gilmore Simms,* sees him as the embodiment of the frontier spirit. Jon Wakelyn, in *The Politics of a Literary Man,* sees him as the architect of secession politics. All see him only partially and in terms of their own special interests. But Simms was not exclusively an inhabitant either of Henry Nash Smith's "Garden" or of Lewis Simpson's "pastoral" world, although there are elements in his work that make possible such readings.

Our passionate search for the roots of twentieth-century agrarianism leads us to a Simms, I fear, that neither he nor his friends would have recognized. And a fuller examination of his writing and his life would prevent such oversimplification. Was he an embodiment of the southern frontier? No. He rejected it more than once, as a boy, as a young man, and in middle age. Was he committed to the southern agrarian economy that Eugene Genovese has persuasively described? No. As editor of the Charleston *City Gazette* he supported what Charlestonians generally then and now contemptuously call "progress": steam and steamboats, railroad developments, national banks, sound currency, and growth of industry. He was even soft on the tariff and opposed nullification, not through reverence for the Constitution but from his belief that the Tariff of Abominations was too small an issue for Draconian measures. Would he have taken his stand with the Nashville Agrarians against industrialism? Probably not. In 1844 he was one of the leaders in the South Carolina Legislature in the fight to pass the act that chartered William Gregg's cotton mill at Graniteville and began southern industrialization. In his arguments on Gregg's behalf he emphasized the South's need for a diversified economy. Simms was a complex and baffling man, and his later reputation has suffered much from the frequency with which he has been fitted into preconceived patterns by his critics. His rich and varied career has deep meaning for those who would understand the nature of the southern experience, as Drew Gilpin Faust has shown in *A Sacred Circle: The Dilemma of the Intellectual in the Old South.* But much of that variety and richness, like the "beauty" of which Gertrude Stein spoke, is lost when Simms is fitted into any fixed pattern, whatever it may be.

A few years ago Louis D. Rubin decided to follow D. H. Lawrence's advice to "never trust the artist . . . trust the tale," and took another and very analytical look at Thomas Nelson Page's story "No Haid Pawn," from the collection *In Old Virginia.* He found some surprising things in the tale, and he concluded: "there are many others like it, stories and poems by southern authors that are potential sources for better understanding of the society and culture out of which they were written. Page's fiction is not, perhaps, in the first rank even of southern literature, but it is the work of an honest and dedicated artist who wrote with skill and perception. And there are others like him."[6] Those are the words of the author of *The Wary Fugitives* about a writer frequently dismissed as the most extravagant of the purveyors of the plantation myth! They should, I think, encourage us, as we look at the writers of both the antebellum and the postbellum periods of the nineteenth century, to set aside our presuppositions and our efforts to demonstrate an inclusive unity in southern writing.

And other new approaches are abroad in the land, and we need to apply them to southern writing—three of them in particular, those of the structuralists and the semiotics, those of the feminists, and those of the students of black culture. These three—although they may ultimately prove as Procrustean as agrarianism and the New Criticism have become—are capable of casting fresh illumination on southern literary culture.

For example, the feminists have already pointed out fresh and valuable elements in Kate Chopin and have done their important part in defining her true place in our letters. What can they tell us about Mary Chesnut, about the Grimké sisters, about local colorists like Mary Murfree, Grace King, Ruth McEnery Stuart, and their numerous sisters? A great deal, I suspect. Certainly the feminists will take fresh looks at the many women writers of the twentieth-century South, and they will probably see new and surprising aspects of their work. Ellen Glasgow is already receiving fresh and exciting attention. Mary Johnston, long dismissed as a dated historical romancer, may well assume a different role as a leading and active feminist of her day. Harriette Arnow should reward the feminist critic richly. What of Elizabeth Madox Roberts, Harper Lee, Julia Peterkin, Lael Tucker, Caroline Miller—to list almost at random some of the nearly forgotten southern women writers? And Katherine Anne Porter, Eudora Welty, Flannery O'Connor, Caroline Gordon—by no means forgotten—probably will be fruitful figures for feminist exploration, and that exploration will certainly qualify and modify the current views of them.

The structuralists and others of the newest European critical schools have already invaded the halls of academe and begun to reshape graduate seminars. So far they have not to a great extent expended their craft in analyzing or deconstructing southern writers, but that is certainly coming. Poe, always the darling of the French, has received the most attention from the phenomenologists, but Simone Vauthier has published studies of works by Simms, John Peale Bishop, Walker Percy, and Marion Montgomery, with interesting results. And, of course, Faulkner, also a darling of the French, is now the object of much of this kind of criticism. Such approaches are certain to alter the general shape of southern literary culture. What I am urging is that we be open to such changes, that we be willing to employ new perspectives in looking at our subject.

And certainly one of the most broadening and enriching of new ways to examine American culture is that offered by the Black Studies movement. It is not merely that we are at last looking at slave narratives, giving Frederick Douglass his long overdue place in southern letters, and examining Charles Chesnutt as an artist rather than a curiosity. A number of writers of great importance are entering the canon—such as Ralph Ellison, Richard Wright, Ernest Gaines, Ishmael Reed. When they enter, they greatly increase the meaning of southern culture, enrich the themes of southern writing, introduce new experiences of their own, and give new perspectives by which to judge the old. The Uncle Remus stories look illuminatingly different when they are examined beside the Uncle Julius stories in Charles Chesnutt's *The Conjure Woman*. Yet old and comfortable categorizing tendencies of southern studies do not respond with ease to these new and vital forces.

There has also been a tremendous amount of excellent work on the southern experience done by historians and sociologists, but our customary definition of literature is too narrow to include much of it. For example, the historical work of C. Vann Woodward and U. B. Phillips has high literary value. The significance of Hinton Rowan Helper's *The Impending Crisis* is cultural as well as historical. The impact of the propagandistic novels of Thomas Dixon, Jr., and particularly of the motion picture *The Birth of a Nation*, may not make us proud but we dare not ignore it. Howard Odum's poetic celebrations and excoriations of the South, in his regional studies and his Black Ulysses trilogy of folk autobiography, are a part of our literary heritage, as is Guy B. Johnson's *John Henry* and his *Folk Culture on St. Helena's Island*. For too long we have ignored these works, to our loss.

Southern writers often lament the effect upon their work of the presence of William Faulkner; to write in his shadow, they say, is like David doing battle with a sling shot, not against Goliath, but against a Sherman tank. But Faulkner's effect upon criticism has been even more devastating. For it has reenforced the widespread modern tendency to value in fiction a kind of romatic impulse and form and to distrust and devalue the realistic mode. That impulse, together with Faulkner's overwhelming example, has led a great many of us—perhaps unconsciously—to exclude a wide and important group of southern writers, those who work in the realistic mode and produce social and social protest novels. The works of these writers, almost without exception, are like Page's fiction, as Rubin saw it, "not in the first rank even of southern literature, but . . . the work of an honest and dedicated artist who wrote with skill and perception."[7] Any study of our literature that neglects T. S. Stribling, Lillian Smith, Erskine Caldwell, Edith Summers Kelley, Dorothy Scarborough, Olive Tilford Dargan, and Grace Lumpkin is presenting a very partial view of the culture and writing of the region. Shields McIlwaine more than forty years ago in *The Southern Poor-White: From Lubberland to Tobacco Road* and Sylvia Jenkins Cook a few years ago in *From Tobacco Road to Route 66* have dealt with skill and sympathy with these writers and others like them, but the standard view of southern writing usually ignores them or dismisses them with a few words.

There has also continued to be produced in the South a kind of novel of manners with a special emphasis on local characteristics and customs, and it too has received relatively little attention from those stunned by the apocalyptic or bowed down before the sacramental—and that includes most of us. We have little difficulty seeing the worth of Augustus Baldwin Longstreet or George Washington Harris or Joseph Glover Baldwin, and we even pay a little lip service to the ghost of George Bagby. That something of the same kind of thing has been done in this century by writers like Marjorie Kinnan Rawlings, Julia Peterkin, Josephine Pinkney, Robert Molloy, DuBose Heyward, James Lane Allen, and even John Fox, Jr., we usually dismiss silently.

Louis Rubin has recently said "The achievement of the twentieth-century South in fiction, poetry, and criticism was not accompanied by a comparable flowering in drama."[8] Although such a statement is basically true, we have most unjustly ignored the significant role that drama has played in southern writing. Indeed, a case can be made that the famed Southern Renascence actually began with drama rather than poetry or fiction, and that, in one sense, it should be dated from the arrival of Frederick Koch at the University of North Carolina in 1918 and the burst of southern folk plays that he encouraged. In 1923 Hatcher Hughes won the Pulitzer Prize for Drama for *Hell-Bent for Heaven;* in 1926 Paul Green won it for *In Abraham's Bosom,* and other playwrights such as Lula Vollmer, best known for *Sun-up,* Lynn Riggs, whose *Green Grow the Lilacs* was the basis for *Oklahoma!,* Laurence Stallings, and Stark Young, made the 1920s and 1930s decades when Southerners were rivaled in the theater only by the graduates of George Pierce Baker's 47 Workshop at Harvard. And in the last four decades Lillian Hellman and Tennessee Williams have been powerful forces in the national theater, perhaps rivalled by Arthur Miller and Edward Albee, but hardly surpassed by them. From the days of the Virginia comedians at Williamsburg in the eighteenth century, the theater has played a significant part in southern culture, but it has seldom received much attention, except in highly specialized studies. In the twentieth century, when the theater in America has at last reached an artistic maturity, it is time to redress the imbalance.

Walter Sullivan, Louis Rubin, and I have debated, perhaps too many times, whether the Southern Renascence has ended. Sullivan has sounded his apocalyptic *Requiem for the Renascence,* and Rubin and I in differing ways have looked more optimistically at the continuity we think we see. But actually Sullivan is correct, if we define southern literature according to Allen Tate's concept of the Renascence—he said, as you will recall, "With the war of 1914–1918, the South reentered the world—but gave a backward glance as it stepped over the border: that backward glance gave us the Southern renascence, a literature conscious of the past in the present."[9] That statement defines Tate's kind of southern literature in the same way that T. S. Eliot's work defines one kind of modernism. There are other kinds of southern writing and of modernism. What I am arguing here is by no means that Sullivan's or Tate's definition of what is *best* in southern writing is wrong; I am only arguing that to confine ourselves to that best is to limit our subject dangerously, to commit ourselves to a past that is surviving only, perhaps, in the work of Eudora Welty, Robert Penn Warren, and Walker Percy, and to shut too many doors to the fresh, the vital, and the new.

By all means let us be glad for the work of Walker Percy, but let us also value that of Harry Crews and William Styron. Let us study, read, and praise Reynolds Price, but let us also see the merit in William Prince Fox. Let us rejoice that we have had Flannery O'Connor and still have Eudora Welty, but let us also be proud of Wendell Berry and Doris Betts.

Let us also remember that critical fashions change with electric quickness. In the 1920s the southern writer eliciting the greatest attention was James Branch Cabell. There were book-length critical studies, genealogies of the characters in his novels, geographical studies of Poictesme, and generally great adulation for him. Who now, anywhere in the wide world—outside the Cabell Society, of course—reads Cabell? Yet we certainly should neither forget nor ignore him, as we have been doing. Nor should we forget the lesson the history of his fame has for us. Who in the 1930s, when his great work was being published in editions of 2,500 copies and not going into second impressions, credited William Faulkner with being our greatest southern writer, much less our greatest American novelist? Read, if you will, what so astute a critic as Alfred Kazin said of him in 1942 in *On Native Grounds,* or look at the amusing review that Clifton Fadiman published in the *New Yorker* when *Absalom, Absalom!* appeared. I am not suggesting that they were right and we are wrong, but I think the record of Faulkner's reputation merits our thoughtful consideration. There is a chance that our judgments of contemporary southern writers—and even our opinion of what is significant about the literature of our region—may look quite as strange fifty years from now as the 1920s judgment of Cabell or the 1930s judgment of Faulkner do to us.

I am not trying to suggest that we modify our critical principles, or that we develop a new southern chauvinism in which we value and praise what is done in the region because it is done in the region. I am not asking for a change in our personal aesthetic or moral or religious values. And I am certainly not trying to renew the old and, it would be nice to think, forgotten war between Vanderbilt and Chapel Hill; I am not seeking to play William Couch to some modern Donald Davidson. What I *am* proposing is that we who are the students and to some degree the custodians of southern literature and culture, in addition to maintaining our critical and moral perspectives, try also to be more historical and descriptive in our treatment of the writing of our region. Let us not canonize our personal tastes and individual values by making them the cards of admission and the frames for analysis of southern writers either of the past or the present. I suppose I am saying, let us be less prescriptive and less proscriptive.

All of us have exercised our common tendency to take the thing we work with and love and to construct out of it a monolithic structure whose proportions will be, we hope, awesome. All of us tend toward the fallacy which Ronald Crane has called "critical monism." But I am trying to suggest that the nature of southern writing is somewhat like Henry James's house of fiction, of which he said:

> The house of fiction has in short not one window, but a million—a number of possible windows not to be reckoned, rather; every one of which has been pierced, or is still piercable, in its vast front, by the need of the individual vision and by the pressure of the individual will. These apertures, of dissimilar shape and size, hang so, all together, over the human scene that we might have expected of them a greater sameness of report than we find. They are but windows at the best, mere holes in a dead wall, disconnected, perched aloft; they are not hinged doors opening straight upon life. But they have this mark of their own that at each of them stands a figure with a pair of eyes, or at least with a field-glass, which forms, again and again, for observation, a unique instrument, insuring to the person making use of it an impression distinct from every other. He and his neighbor are watching the same show, but one seeing more where the other sees less, one seeing black where the other sees white, one seeing big where the other sees small, one seeing coarse where the other sees fine.[10]

The totality of southern writing gives us such a varied report of our region, its culture, and its attitudes. Let us approach it with a deep respect for its richness and variety, its almost endless number of forms and impulses. Let us try to find within ourselves the ability, if not as critics at least as historians, to see Simms and Helper, Page and Glasgow, Longstreet and Reynolds Price, Stribling and Warren, Wolfe and Welty, Tate and the Charleston Poetry Society, Howard Odum and Donald Davidson, Faulkner and Margaret Mitchell, Richard Wright and Thomas Dixon, Joel Chandler Harris and Lillian Smith, Erskine Caldwell and Walker Percy—the whole many-colored multitude of southern writers. And let us say to ourselves and to those who will follow us, *No more monoliths, please!*

Notes

1. Elizabeth Stevenson, *Henry Adams: A Biography* (New York: Macmillan, 1955), p. 360.

2. C. Hugh Holman, "Ellen Glasgow and the Southern Literary Tradition," in *Southern Writers: Appraisals in Our Time,* ed. R. C. Simonini, Jr. (Charlottesville: University Press of Virginia, 1964), p. 123.

3. *Nineteenth-Century Southern Literature* (Lexington: University Press of Kentucky, 1980), pp. 32–49.

4. *Life and Labor in the Old South* (Boston: Little, Brown, 1929), p. 304.

5. "Composition as Explanation," in *Selected Writings of Gertrude Stein,* ed. Carl Van Vechten (New York: Random House, 1962), pp. 514–515.

6. "Southern Literature and Southern Society: Notes on a Clouded Relationship," in *Southern Literary Study: Problems and Possibilities,* ed. Louis D. Rubin, Jr., and C. Hugh Holman (Chapel Hill: University of North Carolina Press, 1975), p. 19.

7. Ibid.

8. "Literature," *The Encyclopedia of Southern History,* ed. David C. Roller and Robert W. Twyman (Baton Rouge: Louisiana State University Press, 1979), p. 728.

9. "The New Provincialism," *Essays of Four Decades* (Chicago: Swallow Press, 1968), p. 545.

10. "Preface to *The Portrait of a Lady,*" in *The Art of the Novel,* ed. R. P. Blackmur (New York: Scribner's, 1934), p. 46.

I

Cleanth Brooks

Southern Literature: The Past, History, and the Timeless

The general topic of this volume is the South in transition, the South in a period of change. Change there has certainly been—some of it for the good, and some of it, I should think, pointless and even damaging. Many of the changes that have taken place in the South have been so much like the changes that have taken place elsewhere in the country that in certain superficial ways it could be said that the South has become indistinguishable from other parts of our nation.

But the fact that an airport in the South is essentially like every other airport in this country, not to mention many in Europe, does not really tell very much of importance. That southern television stations broadcast the same programs shown in Minnesota or Maine is, to be sure, a fact of life, but it does not necessarily mean that southerners must talk like Minnesotans or New Englanders. And the predictable uniformity of chain motels across America can be a convenience to travelers without signalling a shift toward regional uniformity.

If the South has kept pace with some of the superficial changes taking place elsewhere in the country, it has nevertheless, in my view, remained unchanged in more fundamental ways, and I am pleased to cite a recent sociological study in support of my position. John Shelton Reed has written a book replete with statistics and tables, along with incisive insights into some of the intangible features of the South that does not rely solely on the number of outside privies or the incidence of pellagra or the median income of farm workers.[1] Reed notes that in areas capable of quantification, the South is much closer to national norms than it once was, but in less tangible features, such as attitudes toward family, religion, place, and history, the South differs from other parts of the country by a margin that seems to be actually increasing. The South, then, though deeply and genuinely American, consititutes something of a subculture in the larger American domain. I am happy to have my own personal estimate of the still identifiable South corroborated by Reed's ably argued study.

My view of the matter has been further fortified by a number of other books that have appeared in recent years, books by scholars who argue that the differences that mark off the South are of long standing and are in fact rooted in the distant past. I am thinking of C. Van Woodward's *The Burden of Southern History* and *North-South Counterpoint;* Eugene Genovese's *The World the Slaveholders Made,* plus his four other books on related subjects; Raimondo Luraghi's *The Rise and Fall of the Plantation South;* Sacvan Bercovitch's *The American Jeremiad;* Ernest Tuveson's *Redeemer Nation;* C. Hugh Holman's *The Immoderate Past;* and Lewis Simpson's *The Dispossessed Garden.* I am very much aware of the contributions to this volume made by Professors Holman and Simpson, and in these pages I write under their correction. I am in debt to them as well as to the other authorities I have cited, and I must be on my guard against misinterpreting them. Yet it is safe, I believe, to say that, though there are important differences among these books, the ones I have named examine traits which set the South apart from the rest of the nation. In particular, they deal with the often deep-seated historical origins of these regional differences.

Further corroboration for these differences comes, of course, from the brilliant outpouring of southern literature through the past sixty-odd years. Such fiction presents the South, old and new, in works of the imagination that bring alive the unique quality of southern life. It is testimony of this kind I particularly want to offer in the present essay. Though space permits me to cite only a few of the twentieth-century authors that the South has produced, I should like to focus on three topics that seem most closely related to the changeless aspect of southern culture. These are a sense of place; a special conception of time that would take account of the past and of the timeless; and an interest and aptitude for narrative that includes a vigorous oral tradition as well as formal narration in stories and novels.

All of these traits, of course, imply a culture that loves to talk, to tell stories, to remember its roots in the past and to cherish its identity with regard to a family or to a larger community, or to the total region which it regards as a homeland. In such a culture, the people will be chary of abstractions—will be more at home with the concrete—and when members of this culture make use of generalizations, they will want to anchor them to actual incidents by way of illustration. One way in which to describe such a culture is to say that it functions very much as a kinship society in which people attempt to maintain a connection with even their more remote cousins. To say all of this is to offer a compact description of southern society.

This fixation on place, the past, and history provides the base on which so many southern cultural relationships rest. It will furnish us with a convenient means for relating southern writing to the culture from which it springs, and which, by and large, it portrays. One might begin with Eudora Welty's fine essay on the importance of place for her own writing. "The truth is," she says, "fiction depends for its life on place. Location is the crossroads of circumstance, the proving ground of 'What happened? Who's here? Who's coming?'—and that is the heart's field."[2] Though Robert Penn Warren has long lived in New England, he has told me on many occasions that he cannot imagine writing a novel about any other region than his native South. And again, there is William Faulkner who, though he was fascinated by World War I and so tried to write about it, yet was able to do his characteristic and certainly his greatest work only by writing about the South, and, more narrowly still, about his own little postage stamp of territory in north Mississippi.

It need not be that way with every artist. Hemingway, the midwesterner, wrote some of his best work about an American living as a stranger, or even expatriate, in Italy, Spain, and France. So we are not here concerned with a rule for every writer. Rather, I am trying to describe a specifically southern trait. Place in the sense in which it has influenced southern literature is, of course, much more than mere spatial extension—a special landscape. A "place" for Miss Welty or Faulkner is rich in memories, associations, and connections with the past. The past itself adds a dimension of living, a dimension that many twentieth-century Americans almost totally lack. For example, most of the principal characters in Saul Bellow's admirable novel, *Mr. Sammler's Planet,* notably lack an awareness of the past.

What is involved here is not simply a capacity to produce historical novels. For the typical sleazy "historical" novel has actually little to do with history and is usually written for readers who simply want a brief excursion into a world that provides a momentary escape from an often drab and lackluster present. In short, for the typical author of a historical romance, the past is primarily useful for providing a colorful background and exotic attire for his characters. The past allows for a sort of fictional costume party. Historical novels of this sort, it must be confessed, are sometimes cranked out by southerners, but serious literary artists are concerned with bringing the past to bear upon the present and with creating a vital interplay of past and present. Human life is felt to have a continuity, and a knowledge of the past can give meaning to the present. I am thinking here both of one's sense of his personal past and a society's sense of its own history.

One of the most eloquent expressions of the first comes from the pen of Eudora Welty. Toward the end of her short novel, *The Optimist's Daughter,* Laurel McKelva is preparing to leave the family home place. The funeral of her father has taken place a short time before, and she is now clearing out her long-dead mother's desk with its faded letters, notebooks, and other relics of her personal life. On this last night of her sojourn in the house in which she has grown up, the many reminders of her parents' lives, now both ended, bring poignantly into Laurel's mind the nature and meaning of the past. They summon up also the memory of her own husband, Phil Hand, who had found life good, but who had died unfulfilled in the Second World War. When morning finally comes, Laurel prepares to return to her home and work in Chicago; but just then Fay, the cheap young woman who had disastrously become Laurel's father's second wife, enters the room. She taunts Laurel for what seems to her a lunatic brooding on the past. "The past," she declares to Laurel, "isn't a thing to me. I belong to the future." Then, Miss Welty writes:

> And it occured to Laurel that Fay might already have been faithless to her father's memory. "I know you aren't anything to the past," she said. "You can't do anything to it now." And neither am I; and neither can I, she thought, although it has been everything and done everything to me, everything for me. The past is no more open to help or hurt than was Father in his coffin. The past is like him, impervious, and can never be awakened. It is memory that is the somnambulist. It will come back in its wounds from across the world, like Phil, calling us by our names and demanding its rightful tears. It will never be impervious. The memory can be hurt, time and again—but in that may lie its final mercy. As long as it's vulnerable to the living moment, it lives for us, and while it lives, and while we are able, we can give it up its due.[3]

The words the author has put in Laurel's mouth are dramatically right, for this is just what the character as developed in this novel would have at this moment said. But they have a universal significance too. The past "can never be awakened." That is true. But the memory can recall it and memory can indeed suffer "hurt, time and again—but in that may lie its final mercy." For, as Laurel reflects, as long as memory is "vulnerable to the living moment, it lives for us, . . . and while we are able, we can give it up its due." There *is* something due to the past, and our humanity is involved in paying to the past its due. This is the enriching and humanizing gift that the past brings to Laurel, and it is important that is should be so, particularly in our present world, which holds so many creatures like Fay McKelva, who proudly boast "the past isn't a thing to me. I belong to the future." So much for what personal and family history may provide, and the southern writer of our century has indeed made much of what he and his art have been nourished by.

I want now, however, to turn to the larger issues of a whole society's concern for its own history. One could illustrate this also from Eudora Welty's work, but I want at this point to bring in other authors by way of illustration—and a large number of other authors would serve my purpose—Faulkner, Warren, O'Connor, Tate, and many another.

Warren is deeply aware of the present disparagement of history as irrelevant. In an interview published several years ago, he observed that probably at no time before our own day in the United States has history been held in such low esteem. In the contemporary world, he writes, "the contempt for the past becomes more and more marked."[4] Christopher Lasch also has supplied some trenchant comments to the same effect. In a brilliant recent work, he deals extensively with the current disparagement of the past. For example, Lasch refers to "the ever-present sense of historical discontinuity," which he calls "the blight of our society."[5] He defines this "sense of historical discontinuity" as "the sense of living in a world in which the past holds out no guidance to the present and the future has become completely unpredictable" [p. 68]. Christopher Lasch, of course, is not a southerner; but this is precisely why I want to call him in evidence, for I would not have you think that a concern for history as a possible source of wisdom is a truth evident only to southerners.

Back, however, to the southern writers of our time. William Faulkner is the obvious example of a writer with a deep concern for history. Faulkner did not write "historical novels," if we mean by that term escapist fantasies into an imaginary past. Even *The Unvanquished* is much more than a costume romance. It is the story of the intellectual and moral growth of Bayard Sartoris. Bayard does grow up; he has hard choices to make, and the book ends with his having at last achieved self-definition and a firm moral base for his life. For Faulkner, the past was not finished—not over and done with—but vitally alive. Indeed, on numerous occasions, Faulkner has stated that there is no such thing as *was,* that there is no such thing as the past. What he means becomes clear when one reads some of his other utterances on the subject in particular novels. Faulkner saw that for each individual person the past exists only in a present moment of consciousness and, for that matter, so does the future. For the future recedes into the further distance, just as the past does. Yesterday's "tomorrow" becomes "today," just as this present "today" becomes tomorrow's "yesterday." Thus, since our consciousness is always a consciousness in the present, it is in the present moment that both past and present are ingathered.

In taking this position, Faulkner is very close to St. Augustine's perception of the nature of time, though many Faulkner scholars would prefer to claim as his source the French philosopher Henri Bergson. Faulkner did indeed acknowledge a certain debt to Bergson. But in this essay I prefer to go back to that fine phrase which I quoted from Eudora Welty: the memory of the past, if it remains "vulnerable to the living moment," is alive—"lives for us." And if we can be sometimes hurt by memory, we are also nourished by it, for we live not in the minute-to-minute basis of the animals, but in the full and rich dimension of history inhabited by human beings. Moreover, we are products of the past. We have grown out of it, been formed, for good or ill, by its experiences, and willy-nilly, carry a portion of it within ourselves. We may be able to redeem the past—to make good come out of it—or we may perhaps be maimed by it, but it is foolish to believe that we can repudiate the past. This is the truth that most of Faulkner's men and women come to accept. If they fail to accept it, they are indeed lost.

We can extend this perception to the region generally. The South itself has to make the attempt to understand its past, and in doing so, it may come to a true knowledge of itself. As with Eudora Welty's Laurel McKelva, so with the South as a region. In his novels, Faulkner gives us almost every variation on this theme. Some of his characters are victims of the past, people like Quentin Compson or Gail Hightower, who have mistakenly believed that one could escape into the past rather than bring the past to bear meaningfully upon the present. There are also those who, through no fault of their own, find it impossible to make sense of the past, yet courageously, even stoically, carry on into what seems a bleak and hopeless future. I am thinking here of such noble characters as the white woman Judith Sutpen and the black woman Dilsey. One might also name Joe Christmas, who has had any meaningful past ruthlessly snatched away from him and is therefore rendered rootless and alienated from every kind of community, from womankind, from even nature itself. Joe is a truly desperate man, but he never gives up trying to find his own identify.

In Faulkner, there are, to be sure, a few characters like old Bayard Sartoris who are able to bring past, present, and future together in a fruitful relationship. There are also those who deliberately repudiate the past—who would obliterate it totally from their beings: people like the cruel and sadistic Jason Compson, who tries to live in an impossible future; or the abominable Flem Snopes, who seems to have been successful in cutting all ties with the past. Flem registers an almost absolute zero on the human scale. He has no vices, but then he has no virtues, either. He has no appetites—he does not smoke or drink or seem ever to have enjoyed a good dinner. We eventually learn that he is sexually impotent. He has no human warmth—no feeling of any kind. His is an almost reptilian cold-bloodedness. Flem tirelessly makes money. He grasps the farm wife's pittance, the black man's dimes, even the widow's mite. No sum is too small, and Flem snaps them all up as if he were a toad snapping up flies.

To sum up, the southern writers of our century present a culture in which interpersonal relationships are close and important. The family still exists as a normative and stabilizing force. It is culture that is indeed immersed in place and time. Within it, history is vivid and meaningful. Related to the southerner's vivid sense of history and the closeness of his interpersonal relationships is a pervasive religion that undergirds his whole cultural complex. Here again John Shelton Reed's personal insights and his tables of statistics support such a view. His sociological evidence again sets the South apart from the nation in the extent and general uniformity of its religious convictions, which are deeply held and basically orthodox. But for those of you who prefer a literary artist's insight rather than a sociologist's findings, I offer you Flannery O'Connor's fine phrase—"Christ-haunted." Her use of terms is precise: she did not write "Christ-guided" or "Christ-centered," but "Christ-haunted." Even bawdy and rowdy and sometimes roguish southerners cannot quite get the Christ image out of their minds. Jesus is still a presence, threatening or comforting.

This particular artist, a devout Roman Catholic, has quite strict standards of Christian orthodoxy. So has Walker Percy, another Roman Catholic southerner, who writes not only as an artist but also as an intellectual who is intensely interested in the culture of the region. I have in mind his novel *The Last Gentleman.* One of the characters is Sutter Vaught, a physician and member of a prosperous southern family of good stock. But his marriage has gone to pieces, and he has become an alcoholic. Moreover, he has done things that have caused him to be debarred from practicing in certain hospitals.

Were he a clergyman, one could say that he had been defrocked. In short, Sutter has gone to the dogs.

Why then do I quote an utterance from him on the subject of the South? Well, if wisdom sometimes issues from the mouths of babes and sucklings, it can on occasion also be uttered by those who have gone to the dogs. Besides, the passages that I want to cite have to do with pornography. On this subject a very bright, though alcoholic M.D., who knows a good deal about psychiatry and one of whose special hobbies is pornography, ought to qualify as an expert. One of the other characters in the novel discovers that Sutter's case book contains such observations as these: "[In the South] Christianity is still viable enough to underwrite the naughtiness which is essential to pornography (e.g., the pornography of the East is desultory and perfunctory)."[6] In short, Sutter is saying that the reader cannot really get the thrill of being naughty unless he has some residual sense that what he is doing *is* naughty. The next passage reads, "The perfect pornographer = a man who lives both in anteroom of science (not in a research laboratory) and who also lives in twilight of Christianity, e.g., a technician." That is, the honest-to-God working scientist as opposed to the person whose knowledge of science comes from the Sunday newspaper supplements, does not have the makings of the perfect pornographer, nor does the man who lives in the full light of Christianity. But to resume Sutter's definition: "The perfect pornographer = lapsed Christian Southerner (who as such retains the memory not merely of Christianity but of a region immersed in place and time)." Note how neatly this sums up the scheme of southern culture that I have been laboring to present. Sutter continues by saying that the lapsed southerner he has in mind is one "who presently lives in Berkeley or Ann Arbor, which are not true places but sites of abstract activity which could take place anywhere else, a map coordinate; who is perhaps employed as a psychological tester or opinion sampler or computer programmer or other parascientific pursuit. Midwestern housewives, look out! Hand-underdress of a total stranger is in the service both of the theoretical 'real' and the physical 'real' " [pp. 280-281].

Why has Percy said that this perfect pornographer has to be a southerner rather than a New Englander or a midwesterner? Because at least the twilight of Christianity still lingers in the South and because the southerner's religion is still "immersed in place and time." He does not typically live in some "site of abstract activity" like Ann Arbor, Michigan. (I must, by the way, apologize to Ann Arbor, where I once spent a pleasant summer teaching at the University of Michigan; it is not just a "map coordinate." Yet I confess it is much like any other midwestern university town, whereas with Tuscaloosa, Nashville, and Chapel Hill, each does still retain something of its own personality.) Why does Sutter say that his perfect pornographer is "in the service both of the theoretical 'real' and the phsycial 'real' "? Because the southerner still has sufficient knowledge of real places, times, and people for him to hunger for the real. But in an age like our own, in which the old frames of reference have begun to disappear, everything tends to become generalized and abstract. In such a world man comes to feel that the touch of flesh and the sexual act are the only remaining sources of immediate and powerful sensation. Only in sex, he imagines, can he find contact with "real" reality.

I have apologized to Ann Arbor and I apologize to you for bringing up the subject of pornography. That was not merely a ploy to catch your attention but was cited to throw light on southern culture. I am glad to have Walker Percy on my side in maintaining that the South is a region immersed in place and time, with a special history that bolsters its sense of special identity, and a culture that still hungers and thirsts, if not always after righteousness, yet at least after reality.

In any case, Walker Percy's testimony is that of one of our most keen-sighted observers of the present-day South. I take his verdict to be essentially true, even when it is mediated through his alcoholic, pornographic M.D.: because of its special history, religion, and view of reality, the South constitutes a subculture which resembles in its relation to the rest of the country the subcultures of Scotland or Wales to England. Wales, for example, has maintained its separate identity for centuries. So have Scotland and Ireland. But can they continue to do so in this period of tremendous mobility and the electronic media? The answer is that we do not know. And that has to be the honest answer with regard to the South. Yet the stubborn resistance put up by a Scotland or a Wales might be an encouraging sign to those of us who do not want to see the South homogenized into a general American national TV and consumer culture.

Can we learn from these other English-speaking nations? Perhaps, though their situations are markedly different from ours. But even so, we might listen to one of their spokesmen, the poet W. B. Yeats. His essay "What is 'Popular' Poetry?"[7] throws a great deal of light on the nature of contemporary southern literature, though it was not necessarily intended to do so. The essay deals with the oral tradition that produced folk songs, ballads, and folk tales. This tradition was powerful among the Irish people just as the oral tradition has been powerful among our southern folk. Yeats did not think of the unwritten songs and tales told by the folk as in competition with an exalted written literature, but as a force that lived side by side with formal literature and actually gave nurture to that literature.

In the literature of the South this is precisely what has happened. Think, for example, of the semiliterate but vigorous and colorful prose that Robert Penn Warren puts into the mouth of the hillbilly Ashby Windham in his novel *At Heaven's Gate,* or of the wonderful yarns that William Faulkner has V. K. Ratliff spin in *The Hamlet.* Remember in particular Ratliff's story of the wild Texas ponies that Flem Snopes unloaded on the farmers of Frenchman's Bend or his account of Flem's trip to Hell, in which Flem demands an interview with the Devil, whom he outwits and out-talks. Or turn to almost any page of Eudora Welty's *The Ponder Heart* or *Losing Battles* for salty, often witty, and always fascinating talk. In each of these instances, the inspiration, the content, and even the idiom has been borrowed from the oral tradition by an author working in the written tradition. Furthermore, note that these three authors, in spite of their Nobel and Pulitzer Prizes, are not in the least condescending to the unschooled and often ungrammatical speech of the country folk. They recognize literary quality where they see it, and they find in the folk idiom something that is excellent in its own right. The folk speech can be used, obviously, for all kinds of comic effects, but it can be used for serious and even tragic effects also.

What is commonly called popular poetry, however, is as Yeats remarks, not the product of the real folk, at all. In spite of its label, it is really a product of the middle classes and written for consumption by middle-class readers. Who are some of the authors of this kind of literature? Yeats suggests Henry Wadsworth Longfellow, Mrs. Felicia Hemans, and Walter Scott in his longer poems, such as *Marmion* and *The Lady of the Lake*. Where would Yeats today look for examples of this ersatz popular poetry and fiction? I do not know, but I suggest his ghost might find rich pickings in the list of best-sellers in the *New York Times Book Review.*

What cultural situation begets such pseudopopular literature, and who writes it? Here Yeats is very specific: popular literature is written for, and also by, those "who have unlearned the unwritten tradition which binds [together] the unlettered" without ever having taken the trouble to learn "the written tradition which has been established upon the unwritten" [p. 6]. In short, such writers have forsaken the authentic oral tradition with its genuine artistic power and yet have not managed to acquire the mysteries of the high craft that runs from Homer through Dante and Shakespeare down to the true artists of our own day. The result is—and I use Yeats's words here—"the triviality of emotion, the poverty of ideas, [and] the imperfect sense of beauty of a poetry" that one finds typically in a poet like Longfellow [p. 7]. "There is only one kind of good poetry," Yeats declares emphatically, "for the poetry . . . which presupposes the written tradition, does not differ in kind [in range and depth, of course, but not in kind] from the true poetry of the people, which presupposes the unwritten tradition" [p. 10].

The South has had—probably still has—a vigorous unwritten literature sponsored and promulgated through a living oral tradition. In the last sixty years it has also been able to display powerful writing in the written tradition. What ought to worry every southerner, however, is the imminent probability that the unwritten tradition will, in Yeats's terms, be *unlearned* without the written tradition's ever being acquired. This certainly does not mean that those of us who want the South to retain its identity would also like to keep the population charmingly illiterate in order to produce future Weltys and Faulkners, as if southern country folk were to be protected from education like some endangered species fenced off in a human wildlife preserve. Far from it. One does not have to choose between the written and the unwritten traditions. As Yeats has insisted, the two traditions do not compete with each other. And anyone who has ever heard two of our finest southern novelists, Red Warren and Andrew Lytle, drop back into the folk idiom at will as they tell anecdotes and yarns out of their great fund of southern lore, will have had a convincing demonstration that the two traditions can live comfortably within the mind of the same person.

Can a culture that produces such artists as these continue to do so, given the present tendency in America toward patterns of standardization? One certainly hopes so, but it will not be a simple task, what with the steady rise of illiteracy in the nation and the concomitant decline in language study in schools. The existence of both an unwritten and a written tradition of letters—so vital, as Yeats argues, for the health of a nation's literature—calls for teachers willing to study both traditions and capable of teaching both accurately and sympathetically.

What I fear is that the wrong kind of schooling will dilute or replace folk speech with gobbledygook such as educationese, sociologese, and psychologese, all bastard concoctions of a Latinized vocabulary used by people who never studied Latin but who seem to be ashamed of plain English. This synthetic vocabulary is spilled into rambling, broken-backed sentences that wander on and on. The result is a psuedo-English that is not only ugly but often almost meaningless. Surely nobody wants that. Nor do we want merely colloquial English in which the phrase "you know" occurs twice in every sentence. "You know," as it is commonly used, is an appeal to the listener to guess what the speaker is unable to communicate.

I do not mean to rail against southern schooling in particular, and I would like to think that the South would continue to produce great writers. But a South so illiterate and insensitive that it cannot read and admire the Warrens and Faulkners and Tates and Percys and Weltys and Ransoms that it has already produced would be a spiritually impoverished South indeed. It would have become not only ignorant, but dumb—in both the relevant senses of that word: stupid and mute. And that is a danger that confronts both the schools and the culture that sponsors them.

Notes

1. *The Enduring South* (Lexington, Massachusetts: Lexington Books, 1972).

2. "Place in Fiction," in *The Eye of the Story* (New York: Random House, 1978), p. 118.

3. *The Optimist's Daughter* (New York: Vintage, 1978), p. 207.

4. *The Possibilities of Order*, ed. Lewis P. Simpson (Baton Rouge: Louisiana State University Press, 1976), pp. 119–120.

5. *The Culture of Narcissism: American Life in an Age of Diminishing Expectations* (New York: Norton, 1978), p. 50.

6. *The Last Gentleman* (New York: Farrar, Straus and Giroux, 1966), p. 280.

7. *Ideas of Good and Evil* (London: Bullen, 1903), pp. 1–15.

Elizabeth Hardwick

Southern Literature: The Cultural Assumptions of Regionalism

Henry James, in his book on Hawthorne, speaks of the American peculiarity of finding a source of pride in one's mere length of residence in the country. There is likely to be some similar measure of aggressive assertion in the concentration on regional identity. Identity excludes, and "southerness" is a sort of opaque exclusion also. There remains, I hope, some murky distance between the South as a group of states—and not such a clear grouping as I, who was born and educated in Kentucky under the impression that I was living in the South, have reason to know—and the idea of southerness. Many persons who have been in residence in the South for years, decades even, would not describe themselves as southern. Also, one may be a southerner by background and deep experience and yet find himself not a creation of southerness. Not every creative mind living in the region has found itself engaged by that condition. Poe is an example. One of the greatest minds of his time—vivid, original, complicated—his years in Virginia and Maryland do not appear to have been a moral or aesthetic definition. His true home was far away: in Romantic poetry, dark landscapes, brilliant researches and puzzles.

There is culture, custom and attitude, national and personal history; and then there is the self-conscious creation by individual talents of works of the imagination. The South has produced a large, inchoate cluster of images about itself and its place in America. Bad images incline to be more concrete than consoling ones. Racism, with its overwhelming span of social, aesthetic, moral and political details, has been the central image of the South—long after the Civil War, up to our time, the time when it became clear that much of the rest of the country shared in this tragic obsession. Alongside racism in the South there were more acceptable and flattering images, sentimental themes lodged somehow in the old plantation aristocracy. These have had, even in the most unreflective dilution, an astonishing if not always distinguished endurance.

Regionalism itself is a complicated condition for art, particularly for modern art. In its folkloric aspect, it had something to teach us because it valued and honored isolated groups who had lived, spoken, created their manners. In general, for America, the folkloric is exhausted. Except for a unique talent like that of the extraordinarily gifted Zora Neale Hurston, the folkloric is not what we mean when we speak of southern literature.

Writers must live in a place, have families, a youth, and experience in some degree of saturation. This will often, but not always, be a rich part of their creative life. Other sources are the nation, world literature, past and present thought. It is always difficult to judge the weight of the creative resources called upon by an individual talent. Region is one of them—and yet I daresay no ambitious artist wishes to be known as the best painter or novelist in Tennessee, with the mark of the amateurish shining so brightly in the claim to local fame in the arts.

For the South, the burden of fixed ideas in its own mind and in the mind of the country is a hindrance to serious thought and even to the ability to see what is around us. It is not easy to separate oneself from these conventions, conventions that are *high* and *low* we might say—some so commonplace as to be absurd and others more subtle and secretly beguiling. Southerness is more a decision than a fate, since fine talents are not necessarily under any command of place or feeling. Fidelity to place for subject matter is only the beginning of literary art and is seldom as important as the larger claims of intelligence, contemporaneity, freshness, and awareness of the long, noble challenge of literature itself. William Styron's *Sophie's Choice* is a dense and complex example of the southern sensibility meeting modern experience at its most extreme and intractable point: the extermination camps of Germany and Poland. The aspect of this novel that concerns me is the alliance of southern memorics and themes with the making of a literary career in New York, where the action takes place, and the encounter, by way of a central character, with the meaning of the Holocaust.

The southern young man, a writer, the first-person narrator, is close to the author himself, and part of his education from Auschwitz is the discovery of his own subject matter, in this case his novel about Nat Turner. The narrator tells us that he has not forgotten slavery and his own remaining guilt. The scene is the 1950s, and certain plot devices are "excavated" from family events that took place during slavery. The young man in New York is to be saved from bohemian down-and-outness by a legacy that survived from gold buried after an unfortunate sale of a young slave. This small drama in a large and outstandingly ambitious work interested me when I came upon it in my first reading of the book. It seemed to me a lingering refrain from an earlier cavalier tradition sounding its tones among the most urgent reflection on our own time. I use the word "cavalier" very loosely from its source in William R. Taylor's brilliant *Cavalier and Yankee: The Old South and American National Character.* I mean by the word to refer to the presumption of a highly conscious, educated, morally confused, but somehow honorable plantation mind.

Sophie's Choice is suffused with southerness in a number of ways. The guilt of slavery and the guilt of the Holocaust are brought together in the young man's mind. A very curious moment occurs when Sophie is telling of her involvement with Rudolf Franz Höss, the actual kommandant at Auschwitz. Styron turns aside to instruct the reader with information about Höss: "Born in 1900, in the same year and under the same sign as Thomas Wolfe."[1] I think it is best to let that stand as it is, a charming aside of great unlikeliness in other Auschwitz reflections.

The young southern writer, Styron, has his Tidewater memories, his tainted legacy from slavery, but he also has ambitions in the literary world, ambitions as a writer first, and as a southern writer in a world in which a great many vivid figures of his generation are not Southern at all but are instead Jewish. It is not, for example, Eudora Welty that serves as a challenge to his possibilities, but those *others.* With conscious naiveté, never meant to be serious but meant instead to be amusing, there is a scene in which the young writer is asked if he has read Saul Bellow's *Dangling Man.* "Well, dog my cats," he answers. But as the conversation goes on, he begins to feel panic: "Suppose, I thought, the clever son of a bitch was right and the ancient and noble literary heritage with which I had cast my lot had indeed petered out, rumbled to a feeble halt with me crushed ignominiously beneath the decrepit cartwheels? . . . I saw myself running a pale tenth in a literary track race, coughing on the dust of a pounding fast-footed horde of Bellows and Schwartzes and Levys and Mandelbaums" [p. 116]. I include this for its candor, its pedagogical sharpness about the melting pot which is the national literature and in which each talent, from no matter where, churns and turns as he struggles to add his own vision to that national literature.

I am led to another thought by *Sophie's Choice,* this novel so rich in moments of southerness adrift in the contemporary world. The narrator invites Nathan, the Jewish man from Brooklyn, and Sophie, the survivor of Auschwitz, to go to the South with him, to Virginia. He says to them: ". . . at least Southerners have ventured North, have come to see what the North is like, while very few Northerners have really ever troubled themselves to travel to the South, to look at the lay of the land down there" [p. 419].

I wonder what they would see in the South today? Virginia—different indeed from Brooklyn where the novel takes place—but then all places are different from Brooklyn. The landscape of America, from sea to sea, is lizards and moose, oranges and ice floes. The South has its landscape, but that is not what is meant by "seeing the South." The most dramatic region, Florida, is looked upon almost as an outpost of the Caribbean—this long before the Cubans settled there—not "really southern." *Southern* is reserved for others of the former slave-holding states.

So, what will Nathan and Sophie see? "Bad temper, bad manners, poker and treason," in Henry Adams' words? No, they would be on a journey in pursuit of fixed ideas, somehow, somewhere, to find the southern image. Things do not have to be in existence to be imagined as visible. We see what words have told us is to be seen, what popular culture, southern and otherwise, has created. When convention has fixed matters so firmly, even the most diverse, perverse, eccentric, and unaccountable slide into the expected. Films and popular literature will be seen in the South, with the cavalier and the violent passing on the sidewalk.

But what is defining, separating, authentic there? Southern towns have had a place in the literary imagination as vessels of southerness. But the American landscape has altered greatly; people live in such a newness of sight and assumption that the imagination can scarcely take it in without dislocation. The South has seen the same visual and psychological disintegration as the rest of the country and has accommodated the collapse by the same acceptance of the usefulness, the practicality, the inevitability, even the pleasures of the new.

Rural folk with their preserved speech and their dramas of a life with heavy roots gave a special genuineness of tone to southern literature. They, with the rural landscape surrounding them, were there to be used, to be honored, or deplored at times. This was a fixed point. Faulkner, the supreme talent of southern literature, the talent that almost alone gave the literature validity, made the rural South larger than life. Is the rural South still *there,* still somewhat static in its piney isolation, with some of the same woebegone ancestral memories?

It seems to me that the person who would have been in his little farm and shack, like his folks before him getting out the crop, is now in a trailer park, or in his solitary mobile home. Trailers account for almost 80% of low-cost new housing, I have read, and ocular evidence as one travels about the country would not dispute that. The trailer park, the mobile home, is felt by the thoughtful to represent a decline in the national imagination, to be a metallic resting place for the victims of *anomie,* to be a sort of root-killer, depriving of something deeper than the poverty of the old shack with its wisp of wood smoke drifting into the evening sky. No romance, a severing of the old relations abiding between country and town. The cavalier instinct is reduced by the absence of "good country people." Good country people do not grow up on television serials in trailer parks.

The towns of the South, the central cities, with their Main Streets, streets of the small and larger towns alike, are of great importance to the film imagination in its view and idea of the region. Cola drinking, heat, slit-eyed bigots in their pickup trucks with their shotguns on the front seat, sexy, bored young girls, menace, humor, whiskey, majorettes. This is the lower-class white South, visually and culturally a part of the sophisticated American imagination, which makes in turn liberal rejections of what is seen.

It is to the point to wonder what actually remains, whether the shifts in the small-town people have been taken in by themselves as well as absorbed imaginatively by those who would write about them, render them in films and plays. Nothing is harder to keep up with than America. We only know things do not remain the same. New vices, new pretensions, new possibilities, and an altered sense of place in the world—these come about so suddenly, or with what appears to be suddenness, that the literary imagination, slowly taking its shape, finds itself far behind. That is not a defect. Today and yesterday morning are not what literature is about. Still so much has vanished, has been gone for a long time, and to imagine it alive is to trap oneself in banalities.

For the large southern cities, the places of business that once mingled with fine old houses and beaten alleys, the same disintegration has taken place. The rebuilding of downtown Atlanta in recent years is an astonishment. The incredible hotels—in what image are they? Their fake gold chandeliers, the raw orange of the lobbies, the schlock and kitsch of the architecture, the dead shops, the superfluous fountains dripping over plastic rocks: this creation is close to the vision that made Las Vegas out of a wasteland, and very far from the "Old South." The city fathers, the reclaimers of the hallowed "downtown," are like the rest of the country only partly in control of their landscape. But regionalism would not offer an alternative in any case, because the movement of the country is not only stronger than local will, it is stronger than local imagination. There is no way it could be otherwise, and the most refined mind would find it as difficult to create a suitable modern southern architecture as to create a new church. Materials are what we have and what we are. Naturally, the second coming of Atlanta is, among the things one might deplore in the world, not high on the list. It means something, however; it means that the landscape and the people living in it cannot be mythologized in the old way.

The suburbanization of life is another problem for literary southerness. In a suburban world, memories are altered, new fidelities spring up from the streets, if only fidelity to the zoning laws, to the shapes the streets of the suburbs take under the dominion of income and size of building lot. This is family history. One of Peter Taylor's stories expresses a hint of this in a flowing, rhythmical ending. Suburbanization is not the point of the story's plot but rather the consequence of removals from the old ways of life. The persons have cavalier roots in their families, their excellent houses in town, their place in the community. The names, Tolliver and Lila, give the clue. The two people remove themselves from the old town in order to escape their own alcoholism, and here they are:

> . . . Tolliver and Lila just might have the bad luck to live forever—the two of them, together in that expensive house they bought, perched among other houses just like it, out there on some god-forsaken street in the flat and sun-baked and endlessly sprawling purlieus of Memphis.[2]

One solution for the nostalgic southern imagination as it meets a suburban world is to go duck-hunting. This endures in a number of contemporary books, just as it endures in life. Large treasures of southerness are hoarded in the hunting scene: masculinity, drinking, story-telling, memories of the past, of grandaddies and uncles, of country people in the old days, scenes of conflict and consolation. Faulkner, as in everything that relates to this scene of the literary South, is the master of the nostalgic, the historical, the tragic drama that may center upon hunting.

The sentimentalization of the modern South in Tennessee Williams, Truman Capote, and Carson McCullers has an iron hold on the popular imagination, on films, and popular literature. Melodrama, memory, decay, pretension, and dreaming are combined with the tradition of sexual repression, household secrets, and longings. This is dressed up in Williams by attractive vagrants, red-light districts, old rooming houses, aging actresses, offstage strains of jazz: the appeal of the run-down and the heartbroken. For that reason it is difficult when you are thinking about the South to remove your own thoughts from the thoughts put there by the movies.

Walker Percy's *The Moviegoer* is aptly titled. In this cool and memorable novel, the region is bathed in a mist of irony and softened by an acute intelligence very alert to the follies of literary southerness. The young man who goes to movies is a gentleman, well-connected, warm-hearted, and amused by life. He has not done what he was expected to do, to become a doctor or a medical researcher. But, in a very off-hand way, he has taken on the work of a Yankee gentleman—he makes money selling securities. He drives a battered little MG and employs a secretary, a young woman from Eufala, Alabama. And there you have it, the key: the MG and the regional relief of Eufala and the possibility, in the girl, of a vivacious, small-town southern turn of speech. "I'll tell you one thing, son . . . ," she likes to say to her employer, who is also in his casual way her pursuer.

The young man knows about William Holden and Rory Calhoun, but he is a modernist, it turns out, a modernist and a southerner at once. He suffers from what he calls *malaise,* a sort of bearable alienation. He remembers *It Happened One Night,* and in his room he has one book, *Arabia Deserta.* He is very smart, with a very charming and chic volatility of taste. And he has had it with the old French Quarter and the Garden District and instead lives in a suburb called Gentilly, among "old-style California bungalows or new-style Daytona cottages."[3] Tone and the mastery of it are everything in this remarkable book. It is a wicked, contemporary, cavalier creation, careful in detail, balancing effortlessly, or so it seems, on a very thin wire running between the old pieties and a new, fresh southern sensibility.

In only one character does the sophistication falter, and that lies in the presentation of the aunt, with whom the young man has lived. This lingering reminder of the "best of the South" had, we are told, worked in a settlement house in Chicago in her youth, and "embraced advanced political ideas" [p. 26]. Further, she had served as a Red Cross volunteer in the Spanish Civil War before returning home to marry and settle down in the Garden District of New Orleans. Her early "credits" are up-to-date indeed. In that way she has, so to speak, earned her confident articulation of moral nuance, earned a certain surprising intellectuality, and can be the instrument of skeptical analysis combined with "the old forms of civility and even of humor" [p. 219.].

In a long, final rebuke to the young man, the aunt speaks as a sort of philosopher of manners:

> "All these years I have been assuming that between us words mean

> roughly the same thing, that among certain people, gentlefolk I don't mind calling them, there exists a set of meanings held in common, that a certain manner and a certain grace come as naturally as breathing. . . . More than anything I wanted to pass on to you the one heritage of the men of our family, a certain quality of spirit, a gaiety, a sense of duty, a nobility worn lightly, a sweetness, a gentleness with women—the only good things the South ever had and the only things that really matter in this life." [pp. 222, 224]

Moral delicacy and discipline as a social grace, the beleaguered remnants of the old plantation heritage, the sense of *rightness* in Faulkner's lawyer-class, still haunt even the most watchful, observing southern novelists. What may be wondered about is the fineness of the articulation, the lack of temptation to the sloth and ignorance and narrowness of so many of those others who share the presumption of class in the South. In a world where high culture is more and more a specialization, a difficult and mandarin accomplishment left to professors and to writers themselves, it is difficult to imagine the Garden District old lady spending her nights reading the *Crito,* a diversion she mentions in her long speech. I noticed in Eudora Welty's novel *The Optimist's Daughter* that when the father is miserably, restlessly dying, the daughter reads to him from *Nicolas Nickleby.* Eudora Welty and Walker Percy know the reading habits of Mississippi and New Orleans, and they are guarded, careful to include in the ornaments of life the usual popular "serious" works; but the temptation to go a little beyond, not to break the string, seems at times to represent a kind of regional cultural demand.

The Civil Rights Movement, the sharpening of the sense of identity and purpose in the black population of America, the resistance to definition by whites, makes the open use of race treacherous to the white southern writer of fiction. In modern southern literature, which is all that counts except for a few such as the brilliant Kate Chopin, sympathy for blacks is outstanding, with emphasis on dignity, endurance, and practical wisdom. This is Faulkner's Dilsey, McCullers's Berenice, black characters in Lillian Hellman's plays, black characters on television who seem to come out of Jack Benny's Rochester and the radio. The serving class was the source of acquaintance for the two races; but in the present time it is, for literary purposes, thick with possibilities for misadventure.

Again, Walker Percy is on the alert. In *The Moviegoer* is a butler named Mercer, who is commonly described as "devoted." But the clever young man, the modernist, observes that Mercer's face is in reality as "sulky as a Pullman porter's" [p. 22]. Mercer wants to talk about current events, even though, having spent most of his time waiting on dinner parties, he does not know much about them. So, Mercer is a black man in transition. He is "dissolving," finding no vision of himself, either as an old retainer or as an expert in current affairs, rich enough to sustain his new idea of himself.

Wariness about the representation of black life has been constant in twentieth-century southern literature. One of Ellen Glasgow's novels offers an example of this nervous reluctance to assume:

> . . . they passed hurriedly between the crumbling houses and the dilapidated shops which rose darkly on either side of the narrow cinder-strewn walks. The scent of honeysuckle did not reach here, and when they stopped presently at the beginning of Tin Pot Alley, there floated out to them the sharp acrid odour of huddled negroes. . . . The sound of banjo strumming came faintly from the dimness beyond, while at their feet the Problem of the South sprawled innocently amid tomato cans and rotting cabbage leaves.[4]

Ellen Glasgow is interesting in all respects and especially as an example of southerness turning into a comedy of manners open to the exercise of irony and ambiguity. She showed a positive fondness for many of the things later writers mourned, such as destruction of parts of the old landscape in order to accommodate factories.

Flannery O'Connor, asked about the abundance of freaks in southern fiction, said southerners at least were able to recognize them. Her work is the finest, most original to come out of the South in the last three decades. Her vision is never conventional and is instead transforming, altering the ground of expectation. Her freaks are what we may call *genuine*; they are driven by greed, blasphemy, and low cunning; they are dangerous. They assault the sentiments and the "good country people" banalities and devastate the countryside.

There is no pretension in Flannery O'Connor, as there is in Carson McCullers and Tennessee Williams, that the outlandish is filled with hidden goodness, with romantic isolation, and longing. The appalling exchanges between The Misfit and the grandmother in "A Good Man Is Hard to Find" are exaggerations that are serious. The Misfit is a genuine and recognizable monster who can say, "You can do one thing or you can do another, kill a man or take a tire off his car."[5] He has indeed taken *his* measure of the garrulous, hopeful grandmother: "She would of been a good woman . . . if it had been somebody there to shoot her every minute of her life" [p. 133]. The sourness, the angularity of the conceptions, the purity of the ear and of the style, the way things are—in Flannery O'Connor's work I think you find southern literature that is a devastation of southerness.

Faulkner's art, with its high classical diction and its profound absorption in his region, is nevertheless the most experimental to come out of the South. His work seems to me impossible without the avant-garde experiments of the 1920s in all the arts. The fractured view, the distortions of narrative line, the formal difficulties of his great fictions, are landmarks in twentieth-century literary art, to say nothing of southern fiction.

Regions do not produce art. It seems to visit certain countries almost without preparation. Just as Russia was not thought by Marx and Engels to be the most likely place for the Communist Revolution, it is possible to say that Russia was not *supposed to be* the scene of an astounding outburst of nineteenth-century prose fiction. The mystery of place and art is never-ending. In our time, there is the tragic political disappointment of the South American continent, its inability to govern, to use resources wisely, to make national identities of an honorable shape, to create civilized arrangements between the citizens: out of this has come a literature of surprise and brilliance, works of art that perhaps owe more to Europe than to North America.

So it seems to me that we cannot really concern ourselves with the future of southern literature. The conditions for all literature are unknown, accidental, and unpredictable. The South is as much a part of the television, highway world as any other part of the country. It depends upon all that we are as a nation and is in some way more quick to accept the expediencies of the moment than are other regions—and no matter the conflict with the "idea" of the

South. Acceptance of the assumed and recklessly shifting pieties of American life is sometimes known in the South as patriotism.

Walker Percy, when asked how he would account for so many good southern writers, said it was because "we" lost the War. My question would be: which war among those wars that do not capitalize the noun?

Notes

1. *Sophie's Choice* (New York: Random House, 1979), p. 149.
2. "The Captain's Son," in *In the Miro District and Other Stories* (New York: Knopf, 1977), p. 36.
3. *The Moviegoer* (New York: Noonday Press, 1967). p. 6
4. *Virginia* (Garden City, N.Y.: Doubleday, Doran, 1929), p. 41.
5. *The Complete Stories of Flannery O'Connor* (New York: Farrar, Straus and Giroux, 1971), pp. 130–131.

Noel Polk

The Southern Literary Pieties

At a recent meeting of the Modern Language Association, I attended one of the three sessions on southern literature, primarily because I wanted to hear Eudora Welty, whom I consider America's greatest living writer. On the program with Miss Welty, besides academic "respondents," were a southern journalist who had just published his first novel—a "southern" novel, replete with Alabama hillbillies and kudzu and good ole boys making and running moonshine—and a well-known "southern" novelist. The last read first, from a new novel about (save us!) the Civil War, which, he said, he had researched for two years before beginning to write. He prefaced his reading with the statement—this was about two years ago—that when southerners talk about "the war," they still mean THE WAR, as though somehow the thundering hooves and muskets and cannon of First Manassas and Shiloh were *still* loud enough to shame two world wars, Korea, and Vietnam into silence. I groaned (silently of course, being a southerner and a gentleman), but listened on, trying to believe that he was being ironical; I fear he was not. The passage he read from his novel left me and my companions shrugging "so what"—though I will continue to hope, until I have read the novel, that this was the effect of the reading and not of the writing. The journalist read next and was, in my estimation, a considerable step up from the novelist; he was pleasant and witty, and the passage he read from his work was completely journalistic and fairly entertaining, though he also exploited some well-trodden "southern" paths. Miss Welty, need I say, made the program worthwhile.

After the readings one of the respondents, the author of a popular biography of a southern writer, addressed the group in a honeysuckled southern accent that could have pollinated half a dozen Magnolia Grandiflora. She oohed and aahed for several minutes over our readers, then launched into a predictable spiel in which she rehearsed what have apparently become the ground rules for "southern literature." She remarked how wonderful it was, how privileged we were, to be able to *hear* these southern authors read their works, because everybody knows how oral southern literature is, and how musical the southern accent. She was right on target as regards Miss Welty; but I at any rate had not been aware, as I listened to the other two, of anything particularly musical about either voices or prose; and people who have heard William Faulkner and John Crowe Ransom read their works might quarrel with this as a generalization about southern writers. During the rest of her remarks, the biographer ran through a litany of the "characteristics" of southern literature; she spoke in purest cliché about the oral tradition, about the stable agrarian culture, about the family, the sense of history, the experience of defeat, about the tragic and comic sense of life, and so forth, as if she had just recently discovered them.

The performance of the critics and two of the writers on this program forced me to begin to wonder whether we who participate in the southern literature industry—as writers and publishers and reviewers and critics—have not become more interested in the "southern" than in the "literature"? At least since the publication of *Sanctuary* in 1931 and of *Tobacco Road* in 1932, the reading world has come to expect certain things from southern writers that they do not, apparently, expect from other writers; and I think it is demonstrable that publishers and writers have exploited certain aspects of southern literature and made the whole "genre" into a highly marketable commodity. But I also think it arguable, if not demonstrable, that the term "southern literature" has led us to impose certain limitations on southern writers, to expect certain things of them that we would never dream of expecting from the many fine writers from other parts of this country. Nobody bats an eyelash, for example, when Hemingway sets one novel in France, one in Italy, one in Key West, one in Africa; nobody objects when Henry James moves from Boston to New York to Paris; or when Fitzgerald moves from West Egg to the Riviera to Hollywood. Yet listen to the uproar when Faulkner occasionally deserts Yoknapatawpha County, or when Eudora Welty moves outside of her native Mississippi; these moves, as you know, have been accompanied by a chorus of hoots, if not actually derision (though in the case of *A Fable* there has also been that), as though such moves were acts of gratuitous suicide by these writers who in these non-Mississippi books deliberately cut themselves off from their "place." I am extremely tired of reading books and articles on Faulkner which limit their discussions to "the major Yoknapatawpha fiction"; this seems to me an invidious phrase that imposes severe artistic and intellectual limitations on Faulkner and is, finally, based upon a very real, persistent and completely unjustifiable intellectual condescension toward him. I have elsewhere tried to suggest that two of the stories in Miss Welty's *The Bride of the Innisfallen,* the title story and "No Place for You, My Love," are among Miss Welty's finest, most complex achievements in fiction; both stand, in my judgment, on the top shelf along with the best of her Mississippi stories.[1] On the other hand, I am not prepared to defend any suggestion that *Pylon, The Wild Palms,* and *A Fable* are among Faulkner's greatest achievements, although I am willing to grant Faulkner the fifty years he said it might take before *A Fable* could be understood, and although Professors McHaney, Brooks, and Millgate have taught us that *The Wild Palms* is an important book indeed, and well worth our serious attention.[2]

What I would defend, however, is the proposition that these three books are not necessarily inferior *because* they are set outside Yoknapatawpha. The suggestion that in these books Faulkner's power is vitiated because he is operating outside his home country is not intellectually defensible, and critics who argue this throw themselves right back into the bad old days of Faulkner criticism when it was assumed that this poor benighted white Mississippian, albeit a genius, created his world out of his intuition, not out of his intellect—the "rustic genius" theory which, though long exercised publicly, still sputters along just under the surface of much that passes for Faulkner criticism.

The "rustic genius" theory is also at the bottom of attitudes toward other southern writers, too. In the *New York Times Book Review,* Richard Gilman began his review of Reynolds Price's *The Surface of Earth* with a blanket indictment of southern literature and, indeed, of all things southern:

> Although their number is dwindling, essays and books continue to be written about Southern fiction, as though it were an ongoing cultural reality, inimitable and important. Yet the time is long past when Southern writers were either at the center of American literature or powerful influences on the flanks. However much fiction goes on being produced below the Mason-Dixon Line, whatever the density of its local, florid experience, such writing has only the most marginal place in general consciousness now. That there is no present Southern literary art of any distinctiveness, any special energy or élan, is part of the larger truth that there's no weighty, alluring regional literature . . . being created anywhere in the United States today.

With such an attitude, how could Gilman like, or even read objectively, *The Surface of Earth?* He is not, of course, reading that novel, but is reading "Southern Literature," and the underlying though unstated assumption of his review is that Price does not have the intelligence, the hard intellect, to deal with other than these anachronistic, outmoded, unfashionable, down-home themes:

> "The Surface of Earth" comes to us like a great lumbering archaic beast, taking its place among our literary fauna with the stiff queer presence of the representative of a species thought to be extinct. A mastodon sprung to life from beneath an ice-field, it smells at first of time stopped, evolution arrested.
>
> Who could have imagined that any novelist presumably sensitive to the prevailing winds of consciousness . . . could have written a relentless family saga at a time when most of us feel self-generated, inheritors of obliterated pasts?[3]

We can all recognize this for the foolishness it is, for the intellectual dishonesty it represents, and we would all rise in a body to defend *The Surface of Earth* on the purely Jamesian grounds that any writer must be granted his own donnée, as indeed did Miss Welty in a subsequent letter to the editor.[4]

Gilman assumes that southern literature was at one time "at the center of American literature," but that it no longer is. It is as though the "southern writer" can only write from his gut and not from his intellect, that the South has never been anything but the intellectual sahara Mencken called it so many years ago, and that although there are clearly a great many writers down "there" who feel deeply about things, such feeling is no longer enough, since the material has been exhausted, and since the intellect has never been as good as the material.

Gilman's critical and intellectual sin is a serious one. Yet I wonder whether we, as writers and critics, are not sometimes inadvertently on the other side of the same intellectual coin, when as writers we take the easy way out by tapping into the southern literary "conventions" and letting them do our work for us, and when as critics and readers we respond too automatically to those conventions, salivate obediently at the ringing of any of those southern literary bells? The working premise of Gilman's review is that for better or worse southern literature is *different* from *American* literature—different even from *literature,* one suspects—even though the South can no longer be considered so different. Part of the purpose of this volume is precisely to explore the question of whether "southern literature" is indeed a separate but equal, or even unequal, subdivision of American literature, of whether there is a "South" any more distinguishable other than geographically from the rest of America, and of how the relationship between the South and the rest of the world affects the quality of the literature produced by southern writers.

I would take this opportunity to suggest that perhaps the whole idea of the separate southern "place" is too much with us. That, at any rate is what seems to be behind Walker Percy's witty essay, "Why I Live Where I Live." "The reason I live in Covington, Louisiana," he begins,

> . . . is not that it is a pleasant place but rather that it is a pleasant nonplace. Covington is in the deep South, which is supposed to have a strong sense of place. It does, but Covington occupies a kind of interstice in the South. It falls between places. . . .
>
> The pleasantest things about Covington are its nearness to New Orleans—which is very much of a place, drenched in its identity, its

> history, and its rather self-conscious exotica—and its own attractive lack of identity, lack of placeness, even lack of history. Nothing has ever happened here, no great triumphs or tragedies. . .

The entire essay is a very clever potshot at the whole southern notion of place and not without its point. He claims that *places,* as opposed to *nonplaces,* get used up.[5]

I know whereof Percy speaks. His essay manages to articulate something that, without knowing it, I have been trying to explain to myself nearly all my intellectual life. I was born and grew up in a nonplace, a little town in south Mississippi about fifty miles north of New Orleans, and about as far from Covington. It, too, to use Percy's term, was, and probably still is, an interstice in the South. My little nonplace was not a town or even a community or even a watering hole until well into the twentieth century, so we had no statues of Civil War heroes adorning our courthouse square—had no courthouse square, for that matter. We had no huge courthouse or fine "colyummed" antebellum homes sporting minié ball scars which we showed to visitors. I never to my knowledge talked to a Civil War veteran or anybody else who knew one or heard tales about *The War.* There were no Civil War battles that I know of in my area. Andrew Jackson and his merry men seem to have marched through there on the way to fight the battle of New Orleans, but that was in another war and so does not count. Nor was I surrounded by born story-tellers—there was only one uncle who fancied himself one, who invariably stumbled through a joke I had heard at school the day before, and laughed himself into hysterics while repeating the punch line every time his audience's polite laughter subsided. There were blacks, of course, with whom I dealt practically every day, but I recall only one lynching—when Mack Charles Parker disappeared (all but a little bit of him, of course) from the Pearl River County jail, for the alleged rape of a pregnant white woman—but that occurred only in my county, not in my town, and the incident rose up then, as it does now, as an event as atypical to my growing up as a mountain would be in the Mississippi Delta. Otherwise, I am hard put to recall so much as a single act of discourtesy between the races, although lest you rightly accuse me of sentimentalizing, there was of course never any doubt in anybody's mind, white or black, what the racial boundaries were. We were even more of a nonplace, in Percy's sense, in that while living in Mississippi, we were much closer to New Orleans than to Jackson, so we were in a *double* place warp. All our radio, television, and newspapers came from New Orleans; a large part of South Mississippi was virtually cut off from what was going on in our own state. But we had the offsetting advantage of a considerably larger and more sophisticated world view than one could get, in those days, from the media in Jackson. We knew a lot about Louisiana, but not much about Mississippi.

What I am trying to convey, in this specious autobiographical way, is that I, for one deep southerner, did not grow up imbibing from my mother's milk or from my ancestors an overwhelming sense of myself as a *southerner.* When I studied Mississippi and southern history in high school, I might as well have been studying the history of Afghanistan; I *still* cannot keep the names of Confederate and Union generals straight. The air around me was not charged with racial tension, with religious perversion, with scandal, or gossip-mongering about sexually frustrated old maids, or with a sense of the past, or with any of those small-town southern qualities so often represented to us in southern fiction. I seem to have grown up in a history-less backwash of the South, and my life as a southerner is completely out of kilter with the southern life portrayed in fiction. Something is wrong, somewhere.

I hasten to admit that I may simply have been unaware of these things; perhaps they were there and I simply missed them. I also admit that the middle-class mercantile boundaries of my background doubtless insulated me from things I might have known had I been reared either as a sharecropper's son or as the scion of a wealthy father. Let me also admit that the South of my generation might have been, probably was, qualitatively and historically different from the South of previous generations. But even these admissions are part of my general point. I wonder whether my experience is significantly different from that of other southerners, or whether my little nonplace is so completely atypical of the entire South? After all, there are a finite number of Confederate generals and battles and minié balls, and apparently an infinite number of little towns like mine. And I wonder whether the experience of day-to-day life in little southern towns like my own was significantly different from the experience of day-to-day life in equivalent little nonplaces in Ohio and Indiana; our knowledge of human nature might suggest that in many ways they were very similar. So I find myself trying to figure out whether "southern culture" has produced "southern literature" or whether "southern literature" has more potently worked to manufacture a southern culture.

Place certainly works on literature; we have Eudora Welty's eloquent testimony to that. But I am not at all convinced that "southern literature"—or any literature, for that matter—can be explained by historical or cultural circumstances. If it could, then all southern states should have spawned just as many world- and national-class writers as has Mississippi, since for all practical purposes all southern states partook of the same cultural, economic, political, and educational conditions in the hundred years following the Civil War.

In his 1948 review of *Intruder in the Dust,* Edmund Wilson said about William Faulkner and the South the same kinds of silly things Richard Gilman said in 1975 about Reynolds Price and the South: "To be thus out of date," Wilson wrote, "as a Southerner, in feeling and language and in human relations, is, for a novelist, a source of strength. But Faulkner's weakness has also its origin in the antiquated community he inhabits, for it consists in his not having mastered . . . the discipline of the Joyces, Prousts, and Conrads." Here too Miss Welty sprang to the defense not of the South, and not particularly of Faulkner, but of the writer's right to be judged on the basis of his *work* and not on his subject or his home address. Her letter to the editor of the *New Yorker* is a masterpiece of sense and sarcasm, although it is not very well known because she did not include it in her collection of nonfiction: "How well Illinois or South Dakota or Vermont has fared in the *New Yorker* book review column lately, I haven't noticed," she began,

> but Mississippi was pushed under three times in two weeks, and I am scared we are going to drown, if we know enough to.
>
> It's that combination "intelligent . . . despite" that we're given as a verdict each time. The "intelligent" refers to the books or their characters and the "despite" refers to the author's living in Mississippi. Now there's one who is not only intelligent despite, but, it appears, not quite intelligent enough because of. . . . I shy at [Wilson's] idea of novel writing as a competitive, up-to-the-minute technical industry,

> if only for the picture it gives me of Mr. Faulkner in a striped cloth cap, with badge and lunchbox, marching in to match efficiency with the rest only to have Boss Man Wilson dock him—as an example, too—for slipshod bolt-and-nut performance caused by unsatisfactory home address. Somehow, I feel nobody could go on from there, except S. J. Perelman, and he works in another department.

Following this, Miss Welty begins to build toward her main point and I, borrowing from her, toward mine:

> Such critical irrelevance, favorable or unfavorable, the South has long been used to, but now Mr. Wilson fancies it up and it will resound a little louder. Mr. Faulkner all the while continues to be capable of passion, of love, of wisdom, perhaps of prophecy toward his material. Isn't that enough? Such qualities can identify themselves anywhere in the world and in any century without furnishing an address or references. Should this disconcert the critic who cannot or does not write without furnishing his? Well, maybe it should.
>
> Mr. Wilson has to account for the superior work of Mr. Faulkner, of course he has to, and to show why the novelist writes his transcedent descriptions, he offers the explanation that the Southern man-made world is different looking, hence its impact is different, and those adjectives come out. (Different looking—to whom?) Could the simple, though superfluous, explanation not be that the recipient of the impact, Mr. Faulkner, is the different component here, possessing the brain as he does, and that the superiority of the work done lies in that brain? . . .
>
> Nearly all writers in the world live, or in their day lived, out of the U.S. North and the U.S. South alike, taking them by and large and over random centuries. (Only Mr. Wilson is counting for the city vs. the country, to my sketchy knowledge.) And it does seem that in criticizing a novel there could be more logic and purity of judgment than Mr. Wilson shows in pulling out a map.[6]

This letter seems to have been the seed for Miss Welty's well-known lecture/essay of several years later, "Place in Fiction," which has become the classic discussion of the relationship between a writer's "place" and what he writes: "Place in fiction," she wrote, "is the named, identified, concrete, exact and exacting, and therefore credible, gathering spot of all that has been felt, is about to be experienced, in the novel's progress. Location pertains to feeling; feeling profoundly pertains to place; place in history partakes of feeling, as feeling about history partakes of place."[7] But she does not, as many of her followers have done, exaggerate the importance of geographical place. Her opening line is in fact the crucial reminder that

> Place is one of the *lesser* angels that watch over the racing hand of fiction, perhaps the one that gazes benignly enough from off to one side, while others, like character, plot, symbolic meaning, and so on, are doing a good deal of wing-beating about her chair, and feeling, who in my eyes carries the crown, soars highest of them all and rightly relegates place into the shade.

Nevertheless, place, she insists, "can be seen, in her own way, to have a great deal to do with [goodness in writing], if not to be responsible for it." How does place affect writing?

> First, [it has to do] with the goodness—validity—in the raw material of writing. Second, with the goodness in the writing itself—the achieved world of appearance, through which the novelist has his whole say and puts his whole case. . . . Third, with the goodness—the worth—in the writer himself: place is where he has his roots, place is where he stands; in his experience out of which he writes, it provides the base of reference; in his work, the point of view. [p. 117, italics supplied]

Nor is Miss Welty talking only about southern place; she makes no invidious distinctions among novels that are "regional," "American," or even "British," since like James she believes the only valid distinction is that between good novels and bad. If "the local, the 'real,' the present, the ordinary day-to-day of human experience" is the stuff of fiction, it is so, Miss Welty maintains, only after the imagination directs its use. "What can place *not* give?" she asks. "Theme," she answers: "It can present theme, show it to the last detail—but place is forever illustrative, it is a picture of what man has done and imagined, it is his visible past, result. Human life is fiction's only theme" [p. 129]. Miss Welty concludes this essay much as she did her reply to Edmund Wilson, by focusing on the individual writer rather than on the region:

> When I speak of writing from where you have put down roots, it may be said that what I urge is "regional" writing. "Regional," I think, is a careless term, as well as a condescending one, because what it does is fail to differentiate between the localized raw material of life

and its outcome as art. "Regional" is an outsider's term; it has no meaning for the insider who is doing the writing, because as far as he knows he is simply writing about life. . . .

It may well be said that all work springing out of such vital impulse from its native soil has certain things in common. But what signifies is that these are not the little things that it takes a fine-tooth critic to search out, but the great things, that could not be missed or mistaken, for they are the beacon lights of literature.

It seems plain that the art that speaks most clearly, explicitly, directly and passionately from its place of origin will remain the longest understood. It is through place that we put out roots, wherever birth, chance, fate or our traveling selves set us down; but where those roots reach toward—whether in America, England or Timbuktu—is the deep and running vein, eternal and consistent and everywhere purely itself, that feeds and is fed by the human understanding. [pp. 132–133]

It is true that the South is changing; it is true that the outskirts of large southern cities are now indistinguishable from the outskirts of Detroit and Philadelphia and that the South is being pockmarked by an acne of franchise restaurants and motel chains. But I am not terribly disturbed by the change; as Thomas L. McHaney and others have pointed out, the South, like the rest of the country, has *always* been changing, even though we seem now to perceive the twenties and thirties as static years in the South. We are all in transition; change, William Faulkner often said, is necessary, since the only alternative to change is death: it is both inevitable and desirable, even if like William Faulkner we do not believe that all change is necessarily progress. If you want to look on the twenties and thirties in the South, as we look on the sixteenth century in England, as an apex of literary achievement, I have no argument with you; that is your intellectual right. But I must agree with Professor McHaney's suggestion that we should not penalize southern writers who actually have indoor plumbing, nor give extra credit to them if they write about people who do not.[8]

I am not terribly worried, either, about the future of fiction in the South, or in the rest of the country, since like Miss Welty I am not concerned about the future of the imagination, which will nurture itself, somehow, in the right people, regardless of its raw materials. Southern fiction in the future may or may not deal with the

Civil War, with families, with sharecroppers, with racial conflict, with good ole boys. If it is good fiction, we will understand the Civil War and families and sharecroppers and racial conflict and good ole boys as we never have; if it is bad fiction, doubtless it will be hackneyed and formulaic and exploitative and will find its apotheosis as a plot on *The Dukes of Hazzard.* But it will not be good or bad *because* of the subject matter; it will be good or bad only because of the intelligence and the honesty of the artist at work, shaping the material to his own artistic ends.

Part of a writer's place, then, is his hometown, his family, his relationship, or lack of it, to history. But place also includes his imagination, which thrives not just on geography and not just on some conception of The South or Things Southern conveyed to him by generations of ancestors looming from above the mantel, but also on some notion of value, of honor and pity and pride and compassion, which are part of his heritage in the works of Faulkner and Welty and O'Connor and Price and Hardy and Conrad and Tolstoy and Shakespeare and Melville and a myriad of others. "Whatever our theme in writing," Miss Welty has said, "it is old and tried. Whatever our place, it has been visited by the stranger, it will never be new again. It is only the vision that can be new; but that is enough" [p. 133].

Notes

1. "Water, Wanderers, and Weddings: Love in Eudora Welty," in *Eudora Welty: A Form of Thanks,* ed. Louis Dollarhide and Ann J. Abadie (Jackson: University Press of Mississippi, 1979), pp. 95–122.

2. Thomas L. McHaney, *William Faulkner's "The Wild Palms": A Study* (Jackson: University Press of Mississippi, 1975); Michael Millgate, *The Achievement of William Faulkner* (New York: Random House, 1966), pp. 171–179; Cleanth Brooks, *William Faulkner; Toward Yoknapatawpha and Beyond* (New Haven: Yale University Press, 1978), pp. 205–229.

3. *New York Times Book Review,* 29 June 1975, pp. 1–2.

4. *New York Times Book Review,* 20 July 1975, pp. 24–25.

5. *Esquire,* April 1980, pp. 35–36.

6. Quotations from Wilson and Welty in Eudora Welty, "Department of Amplification," *New Yorker,* 1 January 1949, pp. 50–51.

7. *The Eye of the Story* (New York: Random House, 1978), p. 122.

8. Review of *A Requiem for the Renaissance,* by Walter Sullivan, *Mississippi Quarterly* 30 (Winter 1976–1977): 185–188. I am paraphrasing freely, but not, I think, distorting, McHaney's suggestion that Sullivan's argument about the decline of southern literature "almost makes one who would write in and about the South afraid to have running water in his house" [p. 187].

Thomas L. McHaney

Literary Modernism: The South Goes Modern and Keeps on Going

It is doubtful that Modernism, like Ellen Glasgow's realism, crossed the Potomac going north long before anyone noticed. But Modernism was in southern soil early enough; and the literary movement usually called the Southern Renascence was, in reality, a southern branch office of the midwestern division of the North American franchise of that international movement in the arts that flourished in Paris, London, Milan, Munich, and other capitals during the second and third decades of the twentieth century. The southern movement, Lewis Simpson has argued, "has been fully joined in the wider literary and artistic opposition to *modernity*."[1] I would like to discuss this at some length in order to counter the recent lamentations about the end of southern literature, my point being that the Southern Renascence, as unique phenomenon, never existed and therefore as such cannot really end.

Southern experience during the period in question was essentially isomorphic with the experience of the rest of the western world, and it is not surprising, given minds of sufficient talent and will, that southern literature corresponds in many respects to the literature of the larger movement. In a way, the Modern Movement is ironically named, for it was, as Lewis Simpson says, united in its opposition to *modernity*. *Modern* derives from *modo*, "just now," by analogy to the word *hodiernus*, from *hodiea*, "today." It appears first, appropriately, during the Renaissance, another transcontinental movement, and without it we would have had to find a different name for the Quarrel Between the Ancients and the Moderns, a quarrel that we seem engaged upon again in our own time, where the Moderns are, by now of course, the Ancients, and the "now" generation, said to be incapable of matching its forebears, is identified as the Moderns. Modern is simply that which is up to the moment, but the Modern Movement, as we know, is both reactionary and radical, conservative and revolutionary, packaging its puritanism in the latest fashions. The modernists were both the *avante-garde* and the guards of the *derrière,* usually in one and the same person. The Modern Movement is a conservative movement using revolutionary techniques, everything about it implying tension, mediation, paradox.

In *Ulysses, The Waste Land, and Modernism,* Stanley Sultan defines "modernism" simply as that period in twentieth-century letters that felt the impact of the two seminal books of his title. Both works, we know, perform that mediation between past and present that Eliot identified as the "mythical method" in his famous review of Joyce's novel. More generally, Harry Levin has argued that the modernists felt both "belated and up-to-date simultaneously," that they worked "experimental transformations into traditional continuities."[2] Writing about the southerners, Richard James Calhoun expresses a view that explains why it is easy to recognize them as Moderns. They derive their power, he suggests, from a "tension" that existed because of their desire to be unsentimental southerners and, at the same instant, to be technically modern. So far so good, but he goes on to claim that their

> differences from previous Southern writers lay in their dual perspective revealed in their themes and their techniques—on the one hand, their not being completely modern in that they did not feel as fully . . . the historical and metaphysical discontinuities of the most modern writers, while on the other hand they repudiated those traditions and conventions of their Southern past that had mitigated against a significant literature.[3]

I would say that the case was just the opposite. These writers were able to make a significant literature of their traditions and conventions precisely because they felt the historical and metaphysical discontinuities. The error in Calhoun's remarks is that he does not see the southerners as "completely modern." This error, or something like it, is what has prevented many southern scholars from perceiving the so-called Southern Renascence as less than unique. Combined with a natural chauvinism, this view has created a lively trade under the banner "Southern Renascence" and has caused the more recent lamentations for or jeremiads against contemporary southern writing.

Perhaps it is true, as Louis Rubin observes, that this was the "first generation of young southerners since early in the nineteenth century to be brought into direct contact and confrontation with the vanguard of the most advanced thought and feeling of their times."[4] Were they, in this regard, really unique? They were part of a national literary generation, all of whom had grown up under certain cultural and familial pieties, whether they were raised in Oak Park, St. Paul, Reading, Cambridge, or a southern community. They had uncommon perception, all of them, and no one who perceives his own time and place acutely can fail to find discontinuities. They were, in fact, all part of a general "culture of alienation," as Lewis Simpson calls it. Walker Percy's version of what occurred to bring about the modern age and this culture of alienation is a useful one. The age that began about 300 years ago with the dawn of science is over, he says, and along with it, the ways it offered us to explain ourselves. The view that sustained man was

> a viable belief in the sense that it animated the culture and gave life its meaning. . . . something men lived by, even when they fell short of it . . . the belief that man was created in the image of God with an immortal soul, that he occupied a place in nature somewhere between the beasts and the angels.

What has survived and carries current significance in our culture, Percy continues, "are certain less precise legacies of this credo: the 'sacredness of the individual,' 'God is love,' the 'Prince of Peace,' 'the truth shall make you free,' etc." and "a kind of mish-mash view of man, a slap-up model put together of disparate bits and pieces" complemented by the ordinary man's commonsense view of the way science defines him: an organism among organisms.[5]

These definitions no longer work, Percy argues, and those who do not take the matter seriously "forfeit the means of understanding themselves." Those who do take the matter seriously suffer the symptoms of alienation, either wordlessly because they do not know what they feel or, like Percy, by searching for new meanings.

The Modern generation surely felt these discontinuities and engaged in the search for new meaning. The difference between pure alienation and the mood of art, as Percy has written, is the difference between living unconsciously in "the way things are"and knowing how to say "the way things are"[p. 45]. Such consciousness appears to have characterized the artist since the Romantic Movement, however, as our classical American authors reveal. The question is, then, when we regard what has been said about both the uniqueness and the demise of southern writing in the twentieth century, whether or not the consciousness of discontinuities, the search for new meanings, and the general changing can actually ever cease. It seems foolish to think so. If something has ended, then, what exactly is it?

To go back a moment, we can say, first, that the attempt to isolate the so-called Southern Renascence from the Modern Movement gives a false sense of distinctly regional achievement to southern writing. Second, claims that the Renascence is over reflect only the consciousness that the Modern Movement is over, unstated confusion about what that means, and a failure to read the metaphors in contemporary southern work for the current discontinuities they reflect. I will limit myself to some remarks about the Modern Movement and its reported end, hoping that others will be sufficiently interested to take another look at the potential of contemporary southern writing.

The southern writer has had for a long time some of those paradoxical advantages that C. Vann Woodward addresses in *The Burden of Southern History,* though one should not minimize the possibility that America in general, settled by dissidents and radical puritans at the dawn of the age of science, knew more than it was willing to admit publicly about antinomies, paradoxes, and discontinuities. The southern writer also has known for a long time what a scholar like Harry Levin may have discovered only in the 1960s: that despite the freedom of the language in contemporary literature, there is one organ that is rarely dwelt upon—the brain. Ellen Glasgow's observations about Richmond are germane:

> I have always done both my reading and my thinking alone. I have known intimately, in the South at least, few persons really interested in books more profound than "sweet stories." My oldest and closest friends, with the exception of James Cabell, still read as lightly as they speculate, and this description applies as accurately to the social order in which I was born. . . . Nevertheless, as I had discovered in New York and London, the social levels are very much the same everywhere.[6]

As a consequence of his or her own "inner emigration," the southern writer has not needed so much of that literal expatriation that Levin perceives in "What Was Modernism?" as one of the chief preconditions to becoming Modern. Our greatest figures—Glasgow, Faulkner, Welty—traveled significantly outside the South, but they returned to be "underfoot locally," having seen that the country of the mind is a far country indeed, to most people, and one might as well live where one finds the material and can still own a little property. Indeed, staying at home, one is perhaps in a better position to monitor the discontinuities. In the twenties and thirties, there were plenty of discontinuities. Southern society changed, and it has continued to change. But do you suppose it will ever be done changing? It all depends on where you look and who is doing the looking. Glasgow, in fact, could not discern in Faulkner's work a reality that she herself was recording in *The Sheltered Life.* Some of the generation between Faulkner and now cannot discern either the reality or the meaning in people like Cormac McCarthy and Harry Crews. This is not cause for alarm unless writers themselves begin to believe that their countries of the mind, their searches, and their metaphors are not important.

We are in the midst of a Quarrel Between the Ancients and the Moderns, as I have said. Even the defeatist term "Post-Modern" suggests it, something that might have been formulated by J. Alfred Prufrock himself. Prufrock, however, is gone, and one of the things wrong with recent discussions of the end of the Modern Movement is that they focus upon the end of the *beginning* of the Modern Movement without knowing exactly what to make of the fact that Prufrock matured into the persona of the *Four Quartets.* If you reply, "Isn't it pretty to think so?" you should be reminded that Jake Barnes, who was wrong about practically everything and had to leave the waters of San Sebastian, was supplanted by the Old Man of the Sea, and that the suicide Quentin Compson was reincarnated happily as Lucius Priest, whose life-restoring adventure also begins with the death of a grandparent. The gnosticism that is supposed to characterize Post-Modernism exists in the work of Eliot, Faulkner, and Hemingway from the beginning, and it existed in the writing of Melville, Hawthorne, and Poe. The Modern Movement found deep significance in the real, linked the contrarieties, fused the ambiguities, made the mirror and the lamp into a single tool, mediated between past and present, and tried to bridge the supposed vortex between reason and intuition. This impulse is still with us, constantly renewed, and it is that fact that gives me hope—whatever the status of the Modern Movement—that the literary South, like the rest of the literary world, will continue to exist because it will continue to, as I call it, go modern—that is, it will still come up through today to right now, aroused by the discontinuities and able to name them.

We are not exactly born modern. We are born blue and startled like our mothers and our grandparents before us. We become modern when a peculiar consciouness strikes us. The effect may be momentary or lasting; usually, to make an artist, the process must be continually renewed.

In his volume of essays upon language and thought, *The Message in the Bottle,* Walker Percy starts from a moment of *gnosis* of his own. Preoccupied with thoughts about the division between mind and reality and the nature of language—recall Ishmael's desire not simply to meet a horror but to speak it, in order to be on good terms with all the denizens of this world—Percy says he began thinking of the remarkable moment when Helen Keller took possession of the miracle of language-consciousness—words and their relation to things. The moment included an incredible burst of knowledge and also the sudden manifestation of an ethic, a consciousness of regret for some past deeds. Percy is never able to unravel the "Delta-factor," as he calls it, the mechanism by which the connections between mind and thing occur in the act of making language. Whatever it is, he writes, whether "I" or "self" or "some neurophysiological correlate thereof, I could not begin to say" [p. 327].

I cannot say what it is, either, but one realizes that something like this "Delta-factor" is at work not only in the moment of a child's discovery that the patterns of experienced language can be built upon, even retrospectively, but also in the act of making literary art. It is analogous to the condition of "going modern," whether one sees that as the perception of discontinuities and joining the culture of alienation, or simply as speaking, through the consciousness of distance, that which was formerly unspeakable—beauty or horror, love or hate, and other antinomies. Hence the need to find new words and the difficulty of fitting what one has to say to the language one has to say it with. It is not without significance that the Modern Movement has made the paradoxes of physics, biology, and psychology its own, for they lie at the heart of the matter, too, and continue to haunt us. The beginning of the Modern Movement is a revelation to which we have not even begun to apply ourselves because we have been so busy applying ourselves to the forces that set it into motion and the techniques that it discovered to express its vision.

Fiction—poetry, drama, or prose—comes into being in the gap between one's life and one's imagination. The paradoxical truth of fiction depends upon correspondence, upon how truly one finds a metaphor to express one's vision of man's life, and fame depends upon how generally one's metaphor is accepted by thoughtful and sensitive people. Because I believe that this is the way literary art works, I believe there will continue to be southern literary art, and I imagine some of it will be quite good. There is consensus out there waiting to be challenged. Walker Percy says we enter the culture of alienation when we recognize that we, too, have departed from the consensus view of man such as existed in "thirteenth century Europe or seventeenth century New England, or even in some rural Georgia communities today" [p. 18]. But far below the great western theological consensus that he is talking about there are those limited systems into which all of us are born, which many of us discover to be equally invalid, sometimes in ways that produce art. Perhaps it is the loss of the great western consensus that gives us the vision to make this smaller leap, but I doubt it; I think the gap has been perceived ever since man had the luxury and the power of language. As George Santayana said:

> Nature, in framing the human soul . . . unlocked for the mind the doors to truth and to essence . . . partly by endowing the soul with far greater potentialities of sensation and invention than daily life is to call forth. Our minds are therefore naturally dissatisfied with their lot and speculatively directed upon an outspread universe in which our persons count for almost nothing.[7]

What is our compensation? The images that we have made with our hands and our minds. Writers exist to discover language that fills the interstices between the consciousness of reality's potential and reality itself. Call it alienation if you like, and do not minimize the misery that results when the process fails. But trust that in the mysterious interstitial caves of thought there will always be vessels to fill and nourishment to carry back to those few who require or desire it (the news from poems, we know, is hard to get), North, West, East, or South.

Not everyone will agree with me, of course. One of the scientists who is trying to teach language to chimpanzees is hesitant to transmit to them the concept of personal death for fear that the chimps "will deal with this knowledge as bizarrely as we have." He does not want them to have our experience of dread, which, "in the human case, has led to the invention of ritual, myth, and religion"[8]—and one might say, literature. One has to admire his hubris, if not his Godlike restraint. But the real conclusion one draws from this is that they have not gotten very far with their teaching of the chimps, who obviously have not learned to say to one another, "Well, what are we going to do tomorrow?" "What did we do today?" or "Why are we in here and they out there?"

Since we humans seem to be cursed with dread, and hence with ritual, myth, and, if not in all cases religion, literature, one might be tempted to predict what form the next "just-now" literature of the South will take. There will continue to be some use of the grotesque, doubtless, but that is neither the burden nor the triumph of southern writing. Flannery O'Connor's witty remarks to the contrary, southerners are not the last people left who know a freak when they see one, nor are they always able to make the distinction—especially when it comes to politics—while the ability to say what the grotesque means is still a function of art in general. We also know Flannery O'Connor's remark in answer to a question about what kind of novels will be written in the future. The ones that have not been written yet, she said. As Harry Levin said more prosaically, " 'nowness' is a preconditon for newness, for what Whitman had termed 'the unperform'd' " [p. 286]. But Ezra Pound's admonition to "make it new" is also as old as Confucius. The Modern Movement and the so-called Southern Renascence had no monopoly on innovation or renovation; they will always be "what the age demanded."

What does the present age demand of the southern writer? In the culture of alienation there are many mansions. The previous generation was much occupied with the myth of the fall of southern society, a useful myth and an excellent regional metaphor for a world condition. The serpent was not only in the southern garden; he whispered his knowledge of the discontinuities all around. Now the myth is a "Second Coming"—Walker Percy has already preempted the title—and the question is, What rude beast slouches toward Atlanta, Birmingham, Memphis, or New Orleans?

Is the beast so rude? Like Shiloh, Antietam, and Malvern Hill, the names Birmingham, Memphis, New Orleans, and Atlanta are not all happy memories, but they stand, in part, for courage, sacrifice, and pity as much as they do for skyscrapers, parking lots, and fast-food franchises. Things happened in these cities that defy death and humiliation and despoilation of the human spirit. When we see a necessary relation between these two types of battlefields—and, even better, when we recognize that, in all their glory, the events associated with these places also contain the seeds of man's folly and his false pieties—then we will have a new literature.

Edwin Mims predicted in 1920 that "scholarship, literature, and art" would come to flourish in the South—and this is continually coming true. Edwin Alderman once claimed that the southern mind had been the agent to train "the democratic Union for its ultimate victory over the alien system of thought created by southern life."[9] In a strange way, the South has always been the nation's uncreated conscience. It has had its problems, openly. Our national faults and glories have received some of their most vocal and intelligent expression in the South. The South has been dragged into the twentieth century, at last, and the bulldozers have made the approaches to our cities and towns identical with towns in Ohio and California. These things are no more unattractive, however, than the mill village, the town strung along both sides of the railroad tracks, the slovenly wilderness cut by gullies or littered with spilled cotton that did not make it to ramshackle gins and faded compresses in the center of towns devoted to football and nigger-baiting. The collective artifacts of humankind are revealing, proving that the twentieth-century city has no monopoly on greed, litter, poverty, bestiality, or the genteel enclaves from which come the loudest lamentations about the decline and fall of gentility. Having come late to industry, urbanization, science, and a full free expression of the humanities, the South has a better chance to yoke them, to become the conscience of the complex society, not crying from the ruined wall, as some suggest, but walking quietly, reasoning upon important things, in the cooling and clicking garden.

As to subjects, there is much in the South that one returns to, literally or in memory, with the feeling that it is as yet unsung. Our main subjects, however, are ourselves. The concept of the Southern Renascence has had the pernicious effect of convincing some writers, as well as some scholars, that our subject is the Myth of the South, yet both these terms—Southern Renascence and Myth of the South—have reached the status of a "fallacy of misplaced concreteness," the mistaking of the abstraction for the real. What we have is our experience, and, to paraphrase Flannery O'Connor once again, no one who has survived childhood is likely to run out of material to write about. What we must make of our experience is metaphor, and for that we have a world of events and things spread out before us, history and the present age and, always, the changes. The South has gone modern, and it keeps on going.

Notes

1. *The Dispossessed Garden: Pastoral and History in Southern Literature* (Athens: University of Georgia Press, 1975), pp. 65–66.

2. "What Was Modernism?," in *Refractions: Essays in Comparative Literature* (New York: Oxford University Press, 1966), p. 287.

3. "Southern Writing: The Unifying Strand," *Mississippi Quarterly* 27 (Winter 1973–74): 108.

4. *The Writer in the South* (Athens: University of Georgia Press, 1972), p. 105.

5. *The Message in the Bottle* (New York: Farrar, Straus and Giroux, 1975), pp. 18, 19.

6. *The Woman Within* (New York: Harcourt, Brace, 1954), p. 216.

7. "The Prestige of the Infinite," in *Some Turns of Thought in Modern Philosophy* (Cambridge: Cambridge University Press, 1934), p. 120.

8. Quoted by Edward O. Wilson, *On Human Nature* (New York: Bantam, 1979), p. 28.

9. Mims quoted in Rubin, 98–99; Alderman quoted in Robert Bush, "Dr. Alderman's Symposium on the South," *Mississippi Quarterly* 27 (Winter 1973–1974): 16.

Lewis P. Simpson

Home by Way of California: The Southerner as the Last European

The literary difference between the South and West in America is the difference between the literary imagination—or, more broadly, the literary consciousness—as it has manifested itself in the South and in New England. I imply by this somewhat enigmatic statement that the literary destiny of the culture established at Plymouth and Massachusetts Bay in the third decade of the seventeenth century has been the evolvement of the literary consciousness in the American West. I also suggest by negative implication that the culture which began to develop with the founding of Jamestown ten years or so earlier (a less determinable culture in its inception than that of New England) has sought its literary destiny in quite another direction—in an association with the European literary consciousness. Making the latter assertion, even by implication, is, I realize, to disavow an assumption often held by southerners (though scarcely shared by westerners) that the South and West constitute an agrarian community opposed to the industrial North and East. Indeed southerners have at times assumed the West to be an extension of the South.

The authority for this assumption may lie chiefly in one Virginian's westward vision. Dreaming a Canaan more vast than anyone had ever dreamed, Jefferson (partly in secrecy, as much as he was against both secrecy and foreign entanglements) negotiated the purchase of his dream and launched the Lewis and Clark expedition to discover its actuality. Not that the actuality mattered too much in the face of the greater reality of the dream, which embraced the prospect of a thousand generations of self-subsistent yeomen slowly peopling the enormous continental reaches and gradually solidifying a great pastoral republic, forever free from the cities and mobs of Europe. Yet by the time Jefferson died at the end of the first quarter of the last century, his western prospect had been corrupted by the crucial struggle over whether Missouri should be admitted to the new nation as a free or a slave state.

To a degree the aged master of Monticello understood that this crisis in 1820 resulted from a more rapid expansion across the western vastness than he had foreseen; moreover, he understood that the dynamic of this expansion in the nineteenth century arose out of an unprecedented application of technology to nature. But if he had come back to life at the beginning of the twentieth century Jefferson would have been astonished to learn from the census taken in 1890 that his leisurely timetable for the occupation of the western lands (a thousand generations may be estimated to be 20,000 years) had been so drastically disrupted that all the usable free land in America was effectively gone. He would have been further surprised, and disheartened, to learn that a good deal of this space was given to holdings far larger than a respectable freehold and that the hero of the western settlement was not the yeoman farmer of the American pastoral ideal but an idealized frontier wanderer who utterly disdained farming. He would have been still more shocked to learn that this figure, known as a cowboy (a figure fundamentally of Mexican origin and associated with the Spanish imperial conquest of the sixteenth century) had—after the West had become so settled that it had passed into legend, in the year 1902 to be precise—received his apotheotic embodiment in a fictional representative created by a popular author named Owen Wister and known simply as the Virginian.

Although imbued with the Rousseauistic disposition, Jefferson would not easily have understood the association of natural virtue with a man who does nothing but ride across a sublime landscape—whose hands never know a plow handle but only lariat, branding iron, and six-shooter; who spends his time chasing unfenced cattle, lynching cattle thieves, and killing unfriendly Indians (save for the necessary moments when he must duel with colleagues who cheat at poker or speak dishonorably of respectable women, although his usual predilection is for saloon girls who require no defending). Jefferson would have comprehended the part about defending feminine honor. But yoking violence and nature in the production of virtue would have puzzled one reared in a culture in which the tendency, as revealed in a succession of storytellers from William Byrd II to George Washington Harris, was to associate violence in nature with low-life people who lack any capacity for virtue.

Returning to America in 1900, his redoubtable New England co-conspirator in revolution, John Adams, might have understood Owen Wister's concept of the Virginian better than Jefferson; for he would have apprehended in the figure of the cowboy as Wister represents him the fatal motive of the New England character: the zealous and relentless desire to purify history in the name of the autonomy of the individual soul. And in recognizing this motive in the Virginian, Adams, as an omniscient American ghost, would surely have correlated the cowboy not so much with Increase and Cotton Mather as with their heretical yet direct inheritors, the transcendental Emerson and his disciple Thoreau. Indeed the ghostly revisitant might well have made the correlation more exactly with the spiritual son than the spiritual father, calling up a record in which, for instance, the emphasis on self-reliance in "The American Scholar" seems tame compared to that in the chapter on "Higher Laws" in *Walden*.

This noted declaration of selfhood records the twilight moment on the path from Walden Pond, when, glimpsing a woodchuck, Thoreau experienced "a strange thrill of savage delight, and . . . was strongly tempted to seize and devour him raw." "Not that I was hungry then," he says, "except for that wildness which he represented." Thoreau further records that "once or twice" while living at the pond he found himself "ranging the woods, like a half-starved hound, with a strange abandonment, seeking some kind of venison which I might devour, and no morsel could have been too savage for me." Confessing his primal desire, Thoreau distinguishes it as evidence of "a primitive rank and savage" life that is instinctive in him, even though he knows and obeys a "higher, or as it is named, spiritual life." But, Thoreau recognizes, one enters into the higher life through the lower, through an intimacy with nature akin to that known by hunter and trapper. Once, he says, he carried a gun; now he carries a fishing pole but still knows the experience of killing. The "original part" of ourselves, the hunter and fisher, is necessary to the later and higher part. "When some of my friends have asked me anxiously about their boys, whether they should let them hunt," Thoreau remarks, "I have answered, yes—remembering that it was one of the best parts of my education,—*make* them hunters, though sportmen only at first, if possible, mighty hunters at last, so that they shall not find game large enough for them in this or any vegetable wilderness,—hunters as well as fishers of men."[1]

In this cryptic admonition, in which he amends the charge by Jesus to the Galilean fishermen that they be fishers of men to include the idea of being hunters of men as well, Thoreau, ambivalently yet chillingly, identifies the sublimation of the killer instinct in the transcendental aesthetic and ethic. The notable inadequacy of D. H. Lawrence's vision of American types in *Studies in Classic American Literature* is his failure to deal with Emerson and Thoreau; if he had he would undoubtedly have perceived in the austere thrust of the Emersonian-Thoreauvian imperative to psychic dominion and power a remarkable intensification of what he perceives in Cooper's Leatherstocking: the "essential American soul . . . hard, isolate, stoic, and a killer." In Walden Woods Lawrence would have come upon the mightiest of American hunters, the self hunting the self:

> If the red slayer think he slays
> Or if the slain think he is slain,
> They know not well the subtle ways
> I keep, and pass, and turn again.[2]

Perry Miller grimly observes of these familiar lines, "those who shoot and those who are shot prove to be identical . . . in the realm of the transcendental there is nothing to choose between eating and being eaten."[3] Yet in Emerson, and still more in Thoreau, we sense the enactment of a prologue to their entrance into the transcendent unity of the slayer and the slain. On the path to the realm of the Over-Soul they had made a choice, effected a kill: they had murdered the self that is the creature of history and society. The ghost of this murdered creature has not, however, been easily discarded and still haunts Walden Woods. Even though the path to the Over-Soul traverses Thoreau's habitation—and this place is in the best Emersonian sense a natural fact corresponding to a spiritual fact—Walden is, even as he celebrates it, a confinement for Thoreau. He dreams of getting utterly away from any semblance of the self of history, of taking a pure and undefiled path to the westward—of entering into "absolute freedom and wildness, as contrasted with freedom and culture merely civil"; of becoming "an inhabitant, or a part and parcel of Nature." Following a "subtle magnetism in Nature," Thoreau always finds himself heading "between west and south-west." The "future lies that way," he declares. "I must walk toward Oregon, not toward Europe."[4]

But even Oregon is not going to be enough for Thoreau. Getting there was only the culmination of crossing the Lethe of the Atlantic. Beyond lies the "lethe of the Pacific," symbol of the ultimate journey out of history into the absolute freedom of the vast inner territory of self: "Explore thyself. Herein are demanded the eye and the nerve. Only the defeated and deserters go to the wars, cowards that run away and enlist. Start now on that farthest western way, which does not pause at the Mississippi or the Pacific, nor conduct toward a worn-out China or Japan, but leads on direct a tangent to this sphere, summer and winter, day, and night, sun down, moon down, and at last earth down, too."[5]

In the New England imagination of the self as expressed in Thoreau, the West and the self are one. The West is imagined as the transfiguration, the literary apotheosis of New England. To document this phenomenon in detail is beyond my present scope; the most prominent among several pertinent sources is a work I have alluded to, Owen Wister's *The Virginian.* The specific image of transfiguration in this story may be taken to be the description of the idyllic month the cowboy spends in the high country with his bride, Molly Woods, the New England schoolmarm, who has presumably been conquered at last by the code of the West:

> They made their camps in many places, delaying several days here, and one night there, exploring the high solitudes together, and sinking deep in their romance. Sometimes when he was at work with their horses, or intent on casting his brown hackle for a fish, she would watch him with eyes that were fuller of love than of understanding. Perhaps she never came wholly to understand him; but in her complete love for him she found enough. He loved her with his whole man's power. She had listened to him tell her in words of transport, "I could enjoy dying"; yet she loved him more than that. He had come to her from a smoking

> pistol, able to bid her farewell—and she could not let him go. At the last white-hot edge of ordeal, it was she who renounced, and he who had his way.[6]

Yet, significantly, we may ask if the white-hot moment of truth is to be identified as the moment when Molly yields to the embrace of the Virginian after his deadly encounter with Trampas? Had not this moment occurred earlier, when she had discovered the Virginian out on the range, lying unconscious by a spring, critically wounded, the victim of an Indian ambush? When the Virginian had regained consciousness and urged her to leave him and flee, she had "glanced at him with a sort of fierceness, then reached for his pistol, in which was nothing but blackened empty cartridges," and thowing these away had drawn six fresh cartridges "from his belt, loaded the weapon, and snapped shut its hinge" [pp. 331–332]. One need not explicate the sexual symbolism in this scene. In the moment of her possession of the pistol and of her resolution to use it, the New England girl "marries" her cowboy lover, needing only for the consummation of the marriage to occur when the Virginian kills Trampas and she can surrender wholly to the Higher Law of the West (or the Law of Nature). On their wedding journey the Virginian and Molly ratify their entrance into the mystical, indivisible, transcendent union of the slayer and the slain. They become part and parcel of the West—of Nature. Their intrinsic union, which exists beyond history, is in Wister's imagination at once the deification of the American self and the incarnation of the nation in the self. In the last pages of the novel, the South, New England, and the West are brought into indissoluble unity. Some thirty-five years after the bloodiest civil war in history, the nation is at last made whole. The ineffable wedding journey through the pure mountain air—its pristine quality enhanced, sanctified by the aromatic incense of gunsmoke—confirms the nation as part and parcel of Nature: as the perfected community—no, the sacred entity—of the slayer and the slain.

The effectiveness of Wister's metaphor of the nation restored and solidified in a triumph of individuation over the contingencies of history is documented by the popular subscription to the archetype of the Virginian throughout this century. Its power is deeply attested by the response the metaphor has evoked in writers less well-known but of a more serious and sophisticated turn than Wister. I am thinking in particular of Robinson Jeffers, a highly self-conscious voice from the farthermost point of the Western coast. Jeffers' primary significance is that his poems react bitterly and with cogent irony to the obvious failure of the nation (and Jeffers would have regarded Wister's novel as illustrative of the failure) to achieve incarnation in a transcendent image of the Western self. Standing against the involvement of America in Europe, yet feeling that America is being overwhelmed by history, Jeffers offers a final, desperate poetic resistance to history. Conceiving a transcendence of history in the repudiation of its carrier, man, Jeffers—in his murky yet compelling advocacy of what he calls "inhumanism" (which envisions the transformation of man into something "not-man")—murders both the historical self and the transcendental self. He leaves, or would leave, only nature—nature purified of man, whose consciousness is the source both of history and of the desire to transcend it. Marking the end of the New England dream of transcendence of history in the westward movement, poems like "Tamar" and "The Women at Point Sur"—dramatizing the agony of Jeffers' effort to transcend history through nature cleansed of man—suggest a striking retrospective revelation of the underlying motive of the whole American transcendental ethos: a struggle on the part of the modern self to survive history. In the end Jeffers comes to an acceptance—reluctant, desperate—of Americans as creatures of history, destined to bear its burden and to survive it. Seeing the "corrupting burden and curse of victory" descending implacably on America in the Second World War, Jeffers asserts in "Historical Choice" (1943):

> Here is a burden
> We are not fit for. We are not like Romans and Britons—
> natural world rulers,
> Bullies by instinct—but we have to bear it. Who has kissed
> Fate on her mouth, and blown out the lamp—must
> lie with her.[7]

It is notable that in this poem Jeffers displays quite directly—as he does in one way or another in all his work—a feeling commensurate with the southern literary sensibility. I mean a feeling for what I take to be the preeminent characteristic of writers of the American South: their imaginative involvement in the drama of the modern endeavor to conceive of, and to cope with, man as a self-conscious creature of history—as a historical being, a self living altogether in the nontranscendent mode of existence termed secular history. This characteristic of the southern writer—this condition of his imagination—was early established in the way in which the southern colonies became attuned to the radical secularity of the European seventeenth and eighteenth centuries, as opposed to the essential New England continuity with the old European sense of religiosity. This southern secularity, massively documented in Richard Beale Davis' recent *Intellectual Life in the Colonial South, 1585–1763,* accounts for the optimistic and decisive world historical vision of man advanced by Thomas Jefferson.[8] It also accounts for the pessimistic vision of the arrival of democratic man on the stage of world history set forth by a succession of popular southern writers known as humorists. I refer to writers like Augustus Baldwin Longstreet, Johnson Jones Hooper, and George Washington Harris, in whose tales of the frontier South—of the southern West, the Old Southwest (Georgia, Alabama, Mississippi, Louisiana, Tennessee, Arkansas)—the virtuous Jeffersonian yeoman is replaced by Ransy Snaffles, Simon Suggs, and Sut Lovingood. These inversions of the yeoman ideal—all of them conceived by their authors as exemplifications of the historical degradation of civic virtue under democratic circumstances—are followed by Huckleberry Finn. Huck may be taken, as he often has been, as representing the transcendence of democratic virtue. But it takes a pretty determined idealist to see Huck in this light. Defeated by history, he anticipates his later appearance as Niklaus in Mark Twain's *The Mysterious Stranger.* In this story, which translates a frontier South (Missouri) of the nineteenth century to Austria of the Middle Ages, Niklaus and Theodor (Tom Sawyer) encounter a transhuman agency in the angelic nephew of Satan, who reveals not only that the human consciousness of history is a grotesque and foolish dream but that human existence itself is an illusion. But the most interesting aspect of *The Mysterious Stranger* is not its unconvincing attempt to dismiss the human consciousness. Rather it is the reason why Mark Twain translates the historical setting of the Missouri-Arkansas extension of the South into the depths of medieval Europe. Struggling, as Stephen Dedalus was shortly to say in Joyce's *Ulysses,* "to awaken from the nightmare of history," Mark Twain—who, for all his association with the American West, is an untransfigured southerner—finds a means of symbolizing a profound truth, one he fears and resists yet must recognize: the deep American complicity in the long nightmare of European history.

Mark Twain the southerner comprehended a basic truth of American literary history: If the New England destiny has been to assimilate the West to the trancendental vision, the literary destiny of the American South has been to assimilate the West to the historical vision of America as an integral part of the Atlantic and Mediterranean worlds, or, in short, the historic European culture.

I have sometimes thought that the best history of the South, and at the same time the best symbolization of the southern literary imagination, is Faulkner's novel-play, *Requiem for a Nun.* A sequel to *Sanctuary,* this work takes up the further adventures of Temple Drake at the point of a singularly horrible murder. Nancy Mannigoe, Temple's black maid, has killed Temple's baby. Nancy's motive is the salvation of Temple's soul. Exploring this odd and shocking situation, Faulkner entangles us in the complex history of Jefferson and Yoknapatawpha County; and not only in this but in the history of Mississippi, of the United States, and, as a matter of fact, of western civilization, even into its remote ranges. Symbolizing the spiritual history of man, Faulkner subtly juxtaposes the crucial decision Temple makes to return from California—where like many Americans she has fled to escape her history— with the story, told in the prologue to the last act of *Requiem for a Nun,* of Cecilia Farmer. The jailor's daughter in Jefferson at the time of the Civil War, a girl of "invincible inviolable ineptitude," she has used her grandmother's wedding ring to scratch her name on a window pane in the family living quarters of the jail: *Cecilia Farmer April 16, 1861*. During Sherman's invasion of Mississippi, a lieutenant in a Confederate cavalry unit that is fighting a rearguard action in the streets of Jefferson rushes past the jail and sees "the frail and useless girl musing in the blonde mist of her hair beside the window-pane." The "soldier, gaunt and tattered, battle-grimed and fleeing and undefeated" and the girl look at one another "across the fury and pell mell of battle." Then the soldier is gone, but he comes back after Appomattox, all the way from Virginia. Now riding a mule and carrying a sack of corn acquired in Pennsylvania, he finds the girl still musing at the window-pane with her "significantless name" inscribed on it. He marries her at once, puts her on the mule behind him, and they ride off. But not to "Texas, the West, New Mexico: a new land." The "gaunt and undefeated paroled cavalry subaltern" and the "fragile and workless girl" hurry toward the soldier's farm in Alabama, "to begin a life which was not even simple frontier, engaged only with wilderness and shoeless savages and the tender hand of God, but one which had been rendered into a desert (assuming that it was still there at all to be returned to) by the iron and fire of civilization."[9]

The bearing the tale about Cecilia Farmer—who may be an avatar of Lilith, the demonic first wife of Adam, destroyer of men and murderer of children—has on the story of Nancy and Temple is by no means explicit. One of its effects is to suggest that the American West is an illusion. History is never transcended. The past does not pass, and is never lost, the substance of man's existence being his "invincible and enduring *Was.*" Or as Gavin Stevens says to Temple, "The past is never dead. It's not even past" [p. 92]. Lawyer and moral historian of Yoknapatawpha, Gavin is trying to lead Temple to a moral recovery of her past: to make Was *Is,* to make the Is that exists always in Was luminous with the meaning that inheres in the historicism of consciouness. Gavin is at least partially successful. Temple is left at the end of her story as a survivor of history, of the intricate complicity of the self in Is and Was.

Four or five years before Faulkner published *Requiem for a Nun* he was the publisher's reader for a manuscript by Robert Penn Warren entitled *All the King's Men.* Although he did not like the novel very much, we may wonder a little if Faulkner was not influenced by one incident in it, Jack Burden's flight to California. Whether he was or not, Jack's trip, which is central to his retrospective quest for truth in *All the King's Men,* illuminates Temple's story. In the deity he names the Great God Twitch, Jack discovers the God whom Temple seeks in fleeing to California. Jack finds Twitch after an epic journey westward that ends in "a bed in a hotel in Long Beach,"

> on the last coast amid the grandeurs of nature. For that is where you come, after you have crossed oceans and eaten stale biscuits while prisoned forty days and nights in a storm-tossed rat-trap, after you have sweated in the greenery and heard the savage whoop, after you have built cabins and cities and bridged rivers, after you have lain with women and scattered children like millet seed in a high wind, after you have composed resonant documents, made noble speeches, and bathed your arms in blood to the elbows, after you have shaken with malaria in the marshes and in

> the icy wind across the high plains. That is where you come, to lie alone on a bed in a hotel room in Long Beach, California. Where I lay, while outside my window a neon sign flickered on and off to the time of my heart, systole and diastole, flushing and flushing again the gray sea mist with a tint like blood.

Having "drowned in West," his body "having drifted down to lie there in the comforting, subliminal ooze on the sea floor of History," Jack dreams the "dream of our age": that "all life is but the dark heave of blood and the twitch of the nerve."[10] In the West, the psychic homeland of his age, it is revealed to Jack that his life is entirely innocent of crime and sin. In Twitch's dominion, moral categories do not exist. Relieved of all sense of collusion in history, Jack returns to the southern state (nameless in the novel) from which he has fled after discovering that the girl he loves, Anne Stanton, has become the mistress of Willie Stark, the populist governor who has become a dictator. But after the assassination of Willie, Jack (who has been his hatchet man) comes to see that Twitch is an illusion. He interprets his flight from history as an attempt to escape from the truth that we live "in the agony of will." This truth—the truth that "history is blind, but man is not"—gives the "past back" to Jack. Having followed his compulsion, like the speaker in Warren's poem "Rattlesnake Country," "to try to convert what now is *was*/Back into what *is*," Jack is prepared, in his famous last words, "to go out of history into history and the awful responsibility of Time."[11]

Yet the ending of *All the King's Men* is not conclusive. Out of history into history: is the survivor of history, we may ask, never to be unburdened of history? How much self-conscious complicity in history can the self stand? So far as Warren's imagination responds to the question in subsequent novels—and each represents a strenuous effort to respond—the answer is simply, not too much. Warren's formulation of the response to self and history tends toward the attitude expressed by the soldier in his poem about the Vietnam conflict: "History is what you can't / resign from, but / There is always refuge in the practice / Of private virtue, / Or at least in heroism."[12] Warren never really answers the question left hanging over in Jack Burden's story: whether Jack can carry the awful burden of Time without either returning to the automatism of the Great God Twitch, or discovering that self-will is a god more appealing than Twitch. The conviction that history is blind but man is not is dangerous. It prompts the tempting notion that the self may transcend not only Twitch but all gods and manipulate history according to its own dreams and desires. That he has not imagined another character who takes such an affirmative view toward his own involvement in history as Jack Burden does indicates that Warren became wary of Jack's resolution to be responsible for history. Warren's novels after *All the King's Men* focus on the relationship of self to history, but they tend to leave unresolved the self's knowledge of its terrifying isolation in history. They suggest, moreover, that the self knows that it may not survive modern history.

This imagination of the existentialist self is dramatized more directly in a southern novelist who has come to fruition more recently than Warren, Walker Percy. Indeed, in Percy's novel *Lancelot,* we witness a kind of return of Warren's scion of the Louisiana aristocracy and survivor of history, Jack Burden. But we note that Lancelot is worse off than Jack. A southerner who has made his pilgrimage to California—in spirit if not in body—his spiritual home (he wants to believe at any rate) is among the "nowhere people" who live in the world of Raymond Chandler's hardboiled detective Philip Marlowe, the "crummy lonesome" Los Angeles of 1933; merely his body resides in Belle Isle, his showplace plantation home on the River Road above New Orleans. After having blown up Belle Isle, together with his faithless wife and her lover, and having been committed to a New Orleans nut house for a time, Lancelot is ready to answer the question he has propounded during his incarceration: "What do survivors do?"[13] His reply is that he will become the redeemer of America through what he envisions as the Third American Revolution. He will inaugurate this revolt not in California but in the true ideological and spiritual homeland of America, Virginia, where the First Revolution had its effective beginning, as did the Second Revolution, the South's rebellion against the Union. In the Third Revolution, Lancelot, established in Virginia, will cleanse the Sodom and Gomorrah that America has become:

> It won't be California after all. It will be settled in Virginia, where it started.
>
> Virginia!
>
> Don't you see? Virginia is neither North nor South but both and neither. Betwixt and between. An island between two disasters. Facing both: both the defunct befouled and collapsing North and the corrupt thriving and Jesus-hollering South. The Northerner is at heart a por-

nographer. He is an abstract mind with a genital attached. His soul is at Harvard, a large abstract locked-in sterile university whose motto is truth but which has not discovered an important truth in a hundred years. His body lives on Forty-Second Street. One is the backside of the other. The Southerner? The Southerner started out a skeptical Jeffersonian and became a crooked Christian. That is to say, he is approaching and has almost reached his essence, which is to be more crooked and Christian than ever before. Do you want a portrait of the New Southerner? He is Billy Graham on Sunday and Richard Nixon the rest of the week. He calls on Jesus and steals, he's in business, he's in politics. Everybody in Louisiana steals from everybody else. That is why the Mafia moved South: because the Mafa is happier with stealing than with pornography. The Mafia and the Teamsters will end by owning the South, the pornographers will own the North, movies, books, plays, the works, and everybody will live happily ever after.

California? The West? That's where the two intersect: Billy Graham, Richard Nixon, Las Vegas, drugs, pornography, and every abstract, discarnate idea ever hit upon by man roaming the wilderness in search of habitation. [pp. 219–220]

Although I assume this is not consciously intended by Percy, Lancelot's version of what has happened to the West of the New England imperative, the West of the transcendental cowhand and his six-shooter, is strangely connected with the possibility that while Lancelot appropriately represents the return of Jack Burden, he still more cogently represents a return of Wister's Virginian. Having come back to his spiritual homeland, Virginia, by way of a false spiritual homeland, California, the Virginian reveals himself as he really is: a gone-to-seed version of the southerner as, to use Allen Tate's identification of him, "the last European."[14] Removed from his origin in (according to Wister) the Virginia yeomanry, the Virginian is in his incarnation as Lancelot Lamar—and granting the novel's association between Lancelot Lamar and Lancelot du lac, knight of the Round Table—the southern aristocrat as Roman Stoic. (He is a type of the southerner Percy portrays ironically in a woman, Binx Bolling's Aunt Emily in *The Moviegoer;* and, more directly, in Will Barrett's father in *The Last Gentleman,* both Aunt Emily and Will's father being oblique portraits of Percy's "Uncle Will," William Alexander Percy, author of *Lanterns on the Levee.)* The first European to experience the isolation of the individual in history, the Roman Stoic has returned in modern times in many philosophical and literary guises. In Percy's treatment of him as the southern last gentleman, whose historical prototype is John Randolph of Roanoke but whose character is discernible even in Jefferson, he is, like the Roman Stoic, an intellectual seeking to establish the moral authority of the self in a disintegrated society. In this search he appeals to the wisdom of those who may constitute a society of like minds, a Stoic sensibility of order. Thus Lancelot speaks to Percival (the boyhood friend and priest to whom he addresses the monologue that is the structure of Percy's novel) about the "new order of things" he and those like him will create:

> We? Who are we? We will not even be a secret society as you know such things. Its members will know each other without signs or passwords. No speeches, rallies, political parties. There will be no need of such things. One man will act. Another will act. We will know each other as gentlemen used to know each other—no, not gentlemen in the old sense—I'm not talking about social classes. I'm talking about something held in common by men, Gentile, Jew, Greek, Roman, slave, freeman, black, white, and so recognized between them: a stern code, a gentleness toward women and an intolerance of swinishness, a counsel kept, and above all a readiness to act, and act alone if necessary—there's the essential ingredient—because as of this moment not one in 200 million Americans is ready to act from perfect sobriety and freedom. If one man is free to act alone, you don't need a society. How will we know each other? The same way General Lee and General Forrest would know each other at a convention of used-car dealers on Bourbon Street: Lee a gentleman in the old sense. Forrest not, but in this generation of vipers they would recognize each other instantly. [pp. 156–157]

But, although he dreams of the campaigns of the noble Stoic Emperor Marcus Aurelius Antoninus, Lancelot is a vividly degraded Stoic. Essentially he knows only the godhead of Twitch. Having undergone no spiritual metamorphosis like Jack Burden, he has simply returned eastward bearing the .44 of the Los Angeles private dick instead of the six-shooter of the cowboy. He is a discarnate will wandering the Sun Belt, which, embracing a new political and economic concept of the South and West, stretches from the Carolinas to California: the newest of the New Souths, the newest of the New Wests, the newest of the New Americas, the newest of the New Worlds, the new population center of the nation.

Having blown up one small part of Sodom and Gomorrah and

survived, having discovered through this act that there is "nothing at the heart of evil . . . 'no secret'. . . no flickering of interest . . . nothing at all, not even evil," Lancelot, the Virginian as Louisiana hedonist, is truly "hard, isolate, stoic, and a killer." So, incidentally or not so incidentally, is Anna, the victim of the gang rape whom Lancelot has met in the mad house. Once, as Lancelot says, she has killed enough men to prove to herself that she has not been victimized by them, she will join him in the Shenandoah Valley, and help him make a new world.

The law, Wister's Virginian says, is the one honest man in five hundred miles. Affirming what Jack Burden rejects—that the "dark heave of blood and twitch of nerve" is truth; stripping the motive of the Emersonian honest man of all moral idealism; revealing that the real motive of life is "violence and rape," Lancelot stands as a purely honest man, honest enough to be the only law in three thousand miles.

In his ironic vision of the southerner as the last European, Walker Percy continues and extends the southern imagination of the moral complicity of the individual in history. He continues, we may say, the vein of the southern literary difference, yet as he does so he unites the West and New England and the South. Simultaneously he brings to the relationship between Is and Was a sense—intimated in Warren and in Faulkner, yet far stronger than in either—that this relationship is losing its meaning in the South, and in western civilization. A Kierkegaardian, Percy intimates in the drama of his stories something that Kierkegaard himself never seems quite to have grasped: in the self's motive to be passionately inward, passionately subjective, the self both resists and effects a radical, unprecedented internalization of history. This act on the part of the modern self distinguishes it from the self in any other age. In its knowledge of the Kierkegaardian duality of, on the one hand its freedom, and, on the other its historical finitude, the modern secular self knows an unbearable burden, the burden of history. The self also knows—intuits at any rate—that integral to this burden is its will to survive the burden, even if the self must abrogate history and become God. In Percy's conception of Lancelot there seems to be an allowance for the possibility that Lancelot may forbear the assumption of the godhead. As a southerner—as a self fully conscious of the intricate burden of history—he may, Percy hints, still have the capacity to know the difference between God and self. Lancelot tells Percival, the priest who is the audience for his story, that he will wait a time to give Percival's God a chance. Maybe Lancelot means this; maybe his desire to be God is not uncontrollable. As always Percy places the burden of conceiving the final outcome of his novel on the reader—the existing, or the surviving, reader.

Notes

This essay is dedicated to the memory of Thomas L. Brasher.

1. *The Variorum Walden,* ed. Walter Harding (New York: Twayne, 1962), p. 178.

2. Lawrence, in *The Shock of Recognition,* ed. Edmund Wilson (New York: Doubleday, Doran, 1943), p. 965. The lines from "Brahma" quoted in Perry Miller, "From Edwards to Emerson," in *Errand Into the Wilderness* (New York: Harper Torchbooks, 1964), p. 186.

3. Miller, 186.

4. "Walking," in *The Literature of The United States,* vol. 1, ed. Walter Blair, Theodore Hornberger, and Randall Stewart (Chicago: Scott Foresman, 1953), p. 891.

5. "Conclusion," *The Variorum Walden,* 258-59.

6. *The Virginian* (New York: Grossett and Dunlap, 1945), p. 499.

7. *The Double Axe and Other Poems* (New York: Liveright, 1977), p. 129.

8. Cf. Lewis P. Simpson, "The Act of Thought in Virginia," *Early American Literature* 14 (Winter 1979–1980): 253–68.

9. *Requiem for a Nun* (New York: Random House, 1951), pp. 232, 257–259.

10. *All The King's Men* (New York: Bantam Books, 1955), pp. 309–11.

11. *Selected Poems, 1923–1975* (New York: Random House, 1976), p. 50; *All the King's Men,* 438.

12. "Shoes in the Rain Jungle," in *Selected Poems,* p. 159.

13. *Lancelot* (New York: Farrar, Straus and Giroux, 1977), pp. 25, 37.

14. Allen Tate to Donald Davidson, 10 August 1929, in *The Literary Correspondence of Donald Davidson and Allen Tate,* ed. John Tyree Fain and Thomas Daniel Young (Athens: University of Georgia Press, 1974), p. 230. Cf. Robert Buffington's accounts of the life and thought of the young Tate in "Young Hawk Circling," *Sewanee Review* 87 (Fall 1979): 541–56.

II

Michael Millgate

William Faulkner: The Two Voices

The two voices of my title take their origin from Tennyson's poem, "The Two Voices"—essentially a dialogue between despair and hope, suicide and rebirth, negative and positive thinking, resolved in favor of the latter but in terms which leave one wondering whether the defeated, nay-saying voice might not after all have had the better of the argument. In truth, however, the title need not have "come from" anywhere. It is simply a way of insisting upon the pervasiveness of dialogue, debate, and opposition throughout William Faulkner's work, and at the same time of avoiding a term like "dialectical," with which Faulkner himself would probably have been uneasy, and which suggests in any case a far higher degree of ultimate definition and resolution than most Faulknerian texts either achieve or even pursue.

There is, of course, nothing new in insisting upon Faulkner's characteristic counterpointing of characters, themes, and structural units. Twenty years ago Walter J. Slatoff wrote very perceptively about what he called Faulkner's "polar imagination," his fondness for antithesis and conflict, his frequent ambiguity, his often oxymoronic and densely negative style—as when Hightower, in *Light in August*, compares reading Tennyson to "listening in a cathedral to a eunuch chanting in a language which he does not even need to not understand"[1]—and his apparent determination to frustrate the reader's lust for resolutions. Slatoff himself became in the end frustrated and irritated by precisely those habits of Faulkner's mind which he had so interestingly illuminated, and rather squandered his perceptions by arguing, much too extravagantly, that the "polar imagination" was almost schizophrenic in its intensity, ultimately allied itself with disorder, and reflected "a deliberate quest for failure" on Faulkner' part.[2] It seems to me unquestionable that Faulkner's imagination does indeed tend towards polarization—towards patterns of duality and even multiplicity in his structures, in his demography (by which I mean the configurations of characters within particular texts), and in his handling of questions of moral judgment. I would, however, see that kind of patterning as conscious and controlled rather than simply obsessive (or schizoid). And I would argue that it operated for Faulkner as a kind of exploratory device, directed towards the expression or (better, perhaps) the exposition of complexities that he believed to be inherent in his own experience as a human being who happened to inhabit a particular society and region.

It is in the first place sufficiently clear that Faulkner's novels are characteristically "open" in ways that go beyond the typical open-ended novel of the late nineteenth or early twentieth centuries—*The Portrait of a Lady,* for example, or *The Ambassadors,* or *Lord Jim.* There our interest is focused upon some central figure; and we are finally incited to speculate upon what that figure will do in the unnarrated future, or upon the judgment that should be rendered upon his actions in the presented past. Faulkner's novels are never so narrowly focused; if they seem to be so, that appearance proves on closer inspection to be illusory. *Soldiers' Pay,* untypical in many things, is thoroughly typical insofar as it introduces, and sets off against each other, a whole range of characters from different social backgrounds; it also possesses, in Donald Mahon, an ostensibly central figure who is effectively not there. *Sartoris/Flags in the Dust* is similarly lacking in either a hero or a coherent center. The primary focus on the contrast between the hard self-destructiveness of young Bayard and the soft but scarcely less wilful dissolution of Horace Benbow is blurred not so much by the failure of those two characters ever to meet (many of Faulkner's dialogues are carried on between people who do not meet) as by the proliferation of supplementary oppositions between Miss Jenny and Narcissa, between young Bayard and his dead brother John, between several family groups—Sartorises, Benbows, Mitchells, MacCallums, and the two black families—and even between different generations of the same family, between the living and the dead. Though *The Sound and the Fury* and *As I Lay Dying* attain much greater structural coherence, they again deploy a generous range of characters; and these are often disposed in pairs, or even triples, as embodiments of different psychological traits or philosophical positions—sometimes, as Judith Bryant Wittenberg has recently shown, as autobiographical projections of different facets of Faulkner's own psyche.[3] It would be hard to get a random group of critics to agree upon a candidate for the role of hero in either novel, and if Caddy and Addie can perhaps be claimed as heroines, it is only in a very special sense: like Donald Mahon—like the two John Sartorises of *Flags in the Dust*—neither of them is truly present, and their respective novels revolve precisely upon that absence.

Many of Faulkner's texts are "open" almost in the sense in which one speaks of an open forum or an open debate. They are town meetings of the imagination, loud with the rhetoric of advocacy, complaint, and self-justification. In *The Sound and the Fury* and *As I Lay Dying* the air is full of voices, speaking (it is part of their tragedy) to the reader rather than to each other. *Absalom, Absalom!*, too, is almost deafeningly full of conflicting voices. The clear patterns of opposition between Miss Rosa and Mr. Compson as initial narrators and between Quentin and Shreve as narrative partners simultaneously cut across and interpenetrate the central non-confrontation between Sutpen and Charles Bon and the overarching opposition between Sutpen and Quentin, the man of obsessive action and the boy of self-perpetuated immaturity, the two figures upon whose polarity the central tension of the novel depends—between whom, so to speak, it is stretched taut. Even in novels in which the sense of active altercation is less pronounced, the patterns of opposition and contrast still persist. Many such patterns, large and small, are identified in Thomas L. McHaney's excellent study of *The Wild Palms*;[4] and it is immediately clear, especially in a work which Faulkner himself described as contrapuntal, that Harry Wilbourne is set off against the tall convict, Charlotte against the pregnant woman of "Old Man," and the two narratives one against the other. *Light in August* depends absolutely on the constant interplay not only among Lena Grove, Joe Christmas, and Gail Hightower but also on the implicit cross-references between Lena and Miss Burden, between Joe and Percy Grimm, between Byron Bunch and Lucas Burch, and so on. It is a critical commonplace that *The Hamlet* is given unity by the multiplicity of those crisscrossing contrasts and pairings of character and theme that bind it together as one laces up a shoe. And by the time he wrote *Go Down, Moses* Faulkner was ready to integrate a whole series of apparently distinct oppositions within a single contrapuntal structure, pivoting the whole network of cross-references upon the fourth section of "The Bear" and specifically on that debate in the commissary between Ike McCaslin on the one hand and his cousin Cass Edmonds on the other.

From this point onwards the debate becomes a standard element in almost all of Faulkner's novels. One thinks of the long discussions between Gavin Stevens and Chick Mallison in *Intruder in the Dust*; the play-within-a-novel and inquisition-within-a-play of *Requiem for a Nun*; the set piece confrontation between the Marshal and the Corporal in *A Fable*; the unspoken dialogue between the three narrators of *The Town*; the repetition of that technique in the middle section of *The Mansion*, supplemented by another implicit dialogue between the three sections themselves, entitled Mink, Linda, and Flem. There is even the ghostly presence in *The Reivers* of the figures of Virtue and Non-Virtue, hovering around the vulnerable innocence of the young hero like the Good and Bad Angels in *Dr. Faustus*. Nor is that a farfetched comparison, least of all when the hero is called Lucius Priest. In Faulkner, and especially in the later Faulkner, we seem at times to be witnessing a kind of morality play—or even a sequence of morality plays. Reading *The Wild Palms* is rather like watching a pair of medieval pageant-wagons circling around, presenting in turn the successive stages of their sometimes comic, sometimes tragic, always purposive dramas, one from the Old Testament, the other, dense with parallelism, from the New. (In *As I Lay Dying* we are now on the wagon itself, now watching with the audience—none of whom seem anxious to occupy the front rows.) *A Fable*, self-categorized by its title, is only the most obvious and elaborate expression of a tendency towards moral fable that is arguably latent as far back as *Soldiers' Pay*, or even *Marionettes* and *The Marble Faun*.

One might add, since it is integral to Faulkner's fondness for seeing things from all sides, that most of his characters do turn out to be supplied with both categories of angel. The multiplication of characters, of contrasts, and of potentially available points of view provides a perspective within which the reader is eventually obliged to concede the possibility of making out some sort of sympathetic case for even the most deplorable of Faulkner's failures and villains—for Anse Bundren, for example, and even Jason Compson. So the final chapter of *Sanctuary* extorts, in however equivocal a fashion, a flicker of sympathy for the hitherto loathsome Popeye; so, too, Flem Snopes has his moment of dignity at the conclusion of *The Mansion*. A similar process of gradual, grudging revaluation is often enacted within the text of the novels in the way in which the initial impression of a character (for example, of a Joe Christmas) subsequently proves to be radically inadequate. So, in *Intruder in the Dust*, Chick Mallison arrives at a fuller understanding of Lucas Beauchamp, and even of Old Man Gowrie. But an otherwise admirable figure may in due course reveal serious flaws: Ratliff in *The Hamlet*, for example. And in some cases—most notably those of Ike McCaslin and Gavin Stevens—the reader is constantly swung pendulumlike between approval and disapproval, sympathy and rejection, until he comes to realise that judgment in such instances, perhaps in most Faulknerian instances, may be a matter not of "either/or" but rather of "both/and."

Faulkner's texts, in fact, are not only extraordinarily open, they are also unusually fluid. The moral judgments extorted from the reader by the very need to respond to the actions in which the characters engage (burning barns, murdering middle-aged spinsters, depriving idiots of their favorite cows) are always provisional, pending the next twist of the narrative, the next shift in point of view. Characterization itself is never fixed and finite but always in process, obliging the reader to engage in continual readjustments. It is for such reasons that the episode of the old Frenchman Place and the salted gold hoard is placed at the very end of *The Hamlet*, when the reader has long become comfortable with Ratliff, and Ratliff with himself. Neither remembers until too late the cautionary tale, the hubristic fable, of Ab Snopes and the cream separator which Ratliff had himself told earlier in the novel. What Ratliff discovers is that Flem Snopes is the Pat Stamper of the Yoknapatawphan real estate market. What the reader is reassured to learn, as the judgmental pendulum again swings back a little, is that if Ratliff is capable of the gullibility of the unsoured Ab he also possesses the same rueful humor, his "We even got a new place to dig" corresponding precisely to Ab's comment, as his wife puts the same gallon of milk through the separator for the umpteenth time, "It looks like she is fixing to get a heap of pleasure and satisfaction outen it."[5]

One of the most remarkable instances of the provisionality of characterization in Faulkner is that provided by the successive appearances of Mink Snopes in *The Hamlet, The Town,* and *The Mansion*; and over and above the kinds of opposition I have already discussed are those which proceed from the large-scale dialogue (or counterpoint) which can be said to exist not only between the individual volumes of what is, after all, the Snopes *trilogy* but also between all of Faulkner's novels as they stand side by side within the totality of his *oeuvre* (this is a question interestingly touched upon by Gary Lee Stonum in his recent book).[6] I have spoken on another occasion of the existence of a shadowy trilogy structure linking *Sartoris, Sanctuary,* and *Requiem for a Nun,*[7] and it is certainly possible to discern a close relationship between *The Sound and the Fury* and *Absalom, Absalom!*, even to the point of seeing in Sutpen's death at the hands of a gaunt figure yielding a scythe an ironic reference backwards (or forwards) to Quentin's attempt to defeat time by his suicide in *The Sound and the Fury*. But there would also appear to be complex interrelationships between novels not linked by overlapping characters or narratives—the chiming names of Caddy and Addie, for example, draw attention (as Carvel Collins first pointed out)[8] to an implicit opposition between their two novels as explorations of contrasted family units, the one disastrously vacuous, the other tyrannically assertive—and while such interrelationships lie beyond the scope of this present paper, I would nevertheless tend to see them as yet another facet of the same phenomenon, the same Faulknerian habit of mind.

But I am again discussing early, or earlier, Faulkner; and I know that it is still a widely held view that Faulkner's creative arteries hardened in his, and the century's, fifties, and that he then abandoned the complexities and ambiguities of his early and middle periods in favor of a more or less coherent world view, roughly coincident with that of Gavin Stevens, and consisting largely of the resounding affirmation, and tedious reaffirmation, of unimpeachable moral platitudes. Grossly misunderstood by many of his first critics, Faulkner doubtless sought in some of his later fiction to clarify, to spell out, what in his earlier novels had been deemed obscure. But spelling out often meant, for Faulkner, an intensification rather than an abandonment of previous techniques, and the real substance of his saying did not in any case undergo significant change. There is no obvious discrepancy between the Nobel Prize speech and his private comment to Warren Beck in 1941 that he had been "writing all the time about honor, truth, pity, consideration, the capacity to endure well grief and misfortune and injustice and then endure again."[9] No Faulkner novel probes the problems of moral responsibility, the ambiguities of intention and act, more acutely and painfully than does *Requiem for a Nun.* Nor, as Noel Polk's recent book[10] makes clear, is any Faulkner novel more open-ended. If we persist in misinterpreting, or in failing to interpret, *A Fable,* that is perhaps because of our determination to extract a philosophy—coherent, unitary, definable—from what seems so self-evidently philosophical a work. But Thomas Hardy, another novelist often accused of having a philosophy, always insisted that what he offered was nothing other than "a series of seemings," [11] a set of fragmentary impressions of life and truth as they might appear to different people at different moments. And the issues raised in *A Fable,* although given an unusually elaborate development, are finally thrown out to the reader in almost exactly the same unresolved state as those thrown out at the end of *The Sound and the Fury, Light in August, Go Down, Moses,* and all the rest.

The familiar patterns of opposition and contrast still prevail in *A Fable*; they have simply become more self-conscious and more systematic. The old verities of the Nobel Prize speech are indeed dramatized; but, like those truths evoked by Sherwood Anderson at the beginning of *Winesburg, Ohio,* they are shown as making grotesques of those who seek to live by them. Faulkner kept faith with mankind, and in mankind, but it was a faith, as the Nobel Prize speech itself makes clear, grounded in an unblinking recognition of man's capacity and indeed aptitude for every species of inhumanity and folly. It was not that Faulkner wanted it both ways—he saw that it *was* both ways, or indeed, a multiplicity of ways. His fictional world, crowded with echoing forensic voices, with paired characters, with equivocal heroes and emasculated villains, with contrapuntal structures and unresolved meanings and withheld judgments, is from first to last the embodiment of that vision, the enactment of what he called in the Nobel Prize speech "the problems of the human heart in conflict with itself."[12]

Although the materials and settings of Faulkner's fictional world, are, of course, almost exclusively southern, it would clearly be a gross oversimplification to argue that his characteristic habits of mind—or habits of imagination—were also characteristically southern, directly attributable to his having sprung from and grown up in that extraordinary mass of social, historical, and political contradictions called the South. At the same time, several of those features of his fiction which have been discussed in the first part of this paper can certainly be associated with the necessary self-consciousness of the regional writer, especially of the regional writer who is aware, as Faulkner undoubtedly was, of the strategies, at once richly traditional and perennially vital, of pastoral literature. The sheer density of minor characters in such early novels as *Soldiers' Pay* and *Flags in the Dust* clearly has much to do with the regionalist's need to map his region, establish its particularity, create a world at once purposively symbolic and yet sufficiently populated and landscaped to command the willing credulity of his potential urban readers, to whom the region will specifically, and almost by definition, not be familiar. (Even *Wuthering Heights*, which sometimes gets taught and discussed as though it were a hermetically sealed experiment in technique, covers a remarkably wide sociological range.) The multiplicity of contrasted figures and contending voices arises from that same regional self-consciousness and in particular from the almost inevitable impulse to challenge the standard regional stereotypes. As Hardy deliberately rejected the conventional Victorian identification of rural laborers with a stolid, dim-witted, monolithic figure called Hodge, so Faulkner, as Cleanth Brooks has shown,[13] set out with similar deliberateness to display to the nonsouthern world the rich inner variety of the class of people known collectively as "poor whites."

Faulkner's readiness to temper the presentation of heroes and villains alike may itself have something to do with the regionalist-pastoralist's concern, on the one hand, to avoid paragons of virtue who might seem implausible to his sophisticated urban readership and, on the other, to defend his region against the all-too-ready contempt and dismissal of those same sophisticates. Anyone who has travelled overseas must be thoroughly familiar with the experience of defending abroad the policies of governments to which he is, at home, utterly and actively opposed—and the regionalist-pastoralist is, in a real sense, engaged in "representing" his region in distant places, as Faulkner's fellow townspeople half understood when they complained of his "misrepresentin' " Mississippi. He (the pastoralist) is also fundamentally engaged, of course, in setting off his region against the dominant culture of the court, or of modern urban-industrial society. For Faulkner, as a southerner, the sense of that distinctiveness was peculiarly and painfully acute. He was a member not merely of a minority culture but of a rejected culture, a culture which had in one sense been given shape and coherence by the very experience of military and political defeat, and which continued to be sustained by its difference from, and opposition to, a dominant culture that was itself too secure in its dominance to concern itself overmuch with anxieties about its own identity.

Often, as one might expect, it is almost impossible to distinguish confidently between what Faulkner owes to his native southerness and what to his adopted pastoralism. The use of the set debate, for example, can be associated with the traditional dialogues of pastoral poetry (particularly with such modern versions as those of Robert Frost), but the prevailing tone and temper of the altercations that recur throughout Faulkner's fiction would seem to owe a good deal to the conventions of southern oratory. So, at least, Faulkner himself suggested when, in an excessively self-critical mood, he told Malcolm Cowley that his style was the result of the experience of writing in solitude together with the complicating factor of "an inherited regional or geographical (Hawthorne would say, racial) curse. You might say, studbook style: 'by Southern Rhetoric out of Solitude' or 'Oratory out of Solitude.' "[14] However that may be, one can perhaps suggest that those factors—historical, political, social, cultural, and economic—which for so long kept the South depressed, and kept it solid, also gave a peculiar intensity and vigor to Faulkner's personal sense of regional identification and hence to the expression of that identification in his work. I am suggesting, in short, that it was just this intensity and vigor which informed the extraordinary amplitude of his regional creation and the extraordinary ambitiousness and extraordinary adventurousness of his exploitation of basic pastoral strategies. It appears, that is to say, to have been a more complex fate to be a Mississippian than either a Vermonter like Frost or a Dorset man like Hardy. Yeats's literary and personal relationship with his native Ireland perhaps offers a closer comparison, as Brooks has suggested,[15] although it is somewhat undercut by Yeats having been a much less consistent and systematic pastoralist.

The difference between writers like Hardy and Frost on the one hand and Faulkner and Yeats on the other I take to be essentially political. For both Hardy and Faulkner, of course, the region is ultimately their material rather than their subject; they speak primarily to nonregional audiences and draw upon regional material as a means of achieving dramatized expression of fundamental human themes and values. But for Hardy, as for Frost, what is distinctively regional belongs already to the past; the old ways and the old speech are dead or dying; the region, as a region, has no real future. So Hardy writes again and again of the lost world of his own childhood. Faulkner, on the other hand, insists (as does Yeats) upon the necessary preservation into the future of a regional distinctiveness which remains, in his own day, a cultural and political reality. Though deeply and painfully aware of the erosion of values and customs, and of the destruction of the environment, Faulkner harks back to the past chiefly in order to bring it contrastively to bear upon the regional present (in *Absalom, Absalom!* for example, or in *Go Down, Moses*). The resulting dialogue between past and present may indeed serve to demonstrate to his (relatively few) southern readers the need to keep in touch with regional roots and to move forward to a regional future built upon acceptance of the best features of the past and rejection of the worst. But it is simultaneously a means of providing his (relatively numerous) nonsouthern, nonrural readers with a multidimensioned presentation of a particular regional society and culture and of drawing attention—through the implicit dialogue between past and present, perhaps supplemented by an explicit debate between such characters as Ike and Cass—to precisely those basic values, surviving or eroding, which his whole regionalist-pastoralist strategy is designed to assert and affirm.

When I was discussing earlier some of the formal features characteristically found in Faulkner's novels—a profusion of oppositions, a lack of heroes and heroines, a tendency towards openness and final irresolution—it may have seemed that such generalizations were much less directly applicable to *The Reivers*, that apparently unintentional but nonetheless felicitous conclusion to Faulkner's career. There we have not only a clear moral resolution, and a victorious hero of almost Victorian proportions, but also a kind of geniality and even serenity that sorts oddly with the anguish of so many of the earlier works, including those specifically evoked within *The Reivers* itself. No doubt increasing age and crowding honors had encouraged Faulkner to look back upon his own handiwork and see that it was good. He may even have felt that he had, in Lawrence's phrase, come through, in creative and even in personal terms. It seems significant, however, that *The Reivers*, though so clearly Yoknapatawphan and autobiographical in its inspiration, should have been written in Charlottesville, Virginia—the South still, of course, but a very different South, older, wealthier, more self-assured, closer (geographically and politically) to the centers of national power, already more at ease with, because less affected by, the changes beginning to sweep over the region as a whole. Faulkner's travels to different parts of the world had strengthened his belief that devotion to locality and region must at some level be subsumed into patriotism, and patriotism in its turn into a kind of internationalism. The speech he gave to the Southern Historical Association meeting in November 1955[16] makes absolutely clear his sense of the need for an ever-expanding human commitment; and by the time he wrote *The Reivers* he seems to have grown altogether more at ease with his matured, if still complex and even ambiguous, view of the world, and correspondingly less exercised about his specifically regional loyalties.

But *The Reivers* is of course a moral fable, just as surely as *A Fable* itself; and it is possible to argue that Faulkner's old habits of opposition and alternation persisted to the last, and that *The Reivers* is properly read as the particular fable—simple, positive, serene—that we are invited to set off against the dark complexities of *A*

Fable, that novel full of slaughter and of suicides. There is a sense, that is to say, in which the opposition of *A Fable* and *The Reivers* represents the dialogue of Tennyson's "The Two Voices" writ large. So seen, *The Reivers* falls into place not as Faulkner's deliberately final word, but as one work among many, expressive of truths, but not of *the* truth. An authentic and indispensable Faulknerian voice, but not the only Faulknerian voice—merely (by which I mean magnificently) another intervention in that long unresolved because irresolvable dialogue of one human heart in conflict with itself, and secondarily with its region, that we know as the Faulkner canon.

Notes

1. William Faulkner, *Light in August* (New York: Harrison Smith & Robert Haas, 1932), p. 301.

2. Walter J. Slatoff, *Quest for Failure: A Study of William Faulkner* (Ithaca, New York: Cornell University Press, 1959), p. 4.

3. *Faulkner: The Transfiguration of Biography* (Lincoln: University of Nebraska Press, 1979), pp. 78, 111.

4. *William Faulkner's "The Wild Palms": A Study* (Jackson: University Press of Mississippi, 1975).

5. *The Hamlet* (New York: Random House, 1940), pp. 412, 53.

6. *Faulkner's Career: An Internal Literary History* (Ithaca, New York: Cornell University Press, 1979).

7. "Faulkner's First Trilogy: *Sartoris, Sanctuary,* and *Requiem for a Nun,*" in Doreen Fowler and Ann J. Abadie, eds., *Fifty Years of Yoknapatawpha: Faulkner and Yoknapatawpha, 1979* (Jackson: University Press of Mississippi, 1980), pp. 90–109.

8. "The Pairing of *The Sound and the Fury* and *As I Lay Dying,*" *Princeton University Library Chronicle* 18 (Spring 1957): 114–23.

9. William Faulkner, *Selected Letters*, ed. Joseph Blotner (New York: Random House, 1977), p. 142.

10. *Faulkner's "Requiem for a Nun": A Critical Study* (Bloomington: Indiana University Press, 1981).

11. *Jude the Obscure* (London: Macmillan, 1912), p. viii.

12. *Essays, Speeches & Public Letters*, ed. James B. Meriwether (New York: Random House, 1967), p. 119.

13. *William Faulkner: The Yoknapatawpha Country* (New Haven: Yale University Press, 1963), pp. 10–28.

14. *Selected Letters,* 215–6.

15. Brooks, 2–3.

16. *Essays, Speeches & Public Letters,* 146–51.

William Osborne

John Crowe Ransom: Toward a Pastoral

I

After three years at Oxford as a Rhodes Scholar, John Crowe Ransom, then twenty-five, returned to this country to take a one-year appointment teaching Latin at a boys' preparatory school in Connecticut. The year was 1913, an important one for Ransom, since he would decide not only what occupation to pursue, but also where to pursue it. His father was urging him to return to middle Tennessee, whatever profession he chose to follow. But Ransom had become attracted to the metropolitan Northeast, and he was considering entering an Ivy League university for doctoral studies, going into journalism, or continuing to teach. His letters to his father point up the division in his mind at this time between the advantages, respectively, of country and city.

Indeed, the habit of weighing alternatives and making choices was not new in the Ransom family. In his biography, Thomas Daniel Young stresses the importance of discussion and debate to Ransom's father, a Methodist minister, and how young Ransom grew up listening to and later taking on his father in spirited debate.[1] Such debates were to continue with fellow students at Oxford, with the Fugitives in Nashville, and finally with Allen Tate, with whom he engaged in a productive literary correspondence. Both Young and Louis Rubin affirm that for Ransom, debate—oral or written—was an important means of intellectual discovery. Rubin writes: "He was . . . always willing to debate almost any issue at any time; it was his way of thinking."[2]

Though letters written in 1913 show Ransom's love of family and his desire to return home after his long absence, they also suggest a growing sense of the superiority of metropolitan centers over rural areas. In one letter to his father, Ransom reveals a set of ideas about the rural South strikingly at odds with ideas he would defend in his Agrarian years:

> Country conditions operate to produce in country people the quality of stability, conformity, mental and spiritual inertia, callousness, monotony. . . . The country community is very small; very native or inbred and therefore very homogeneous, and very well fortified against the intrusion of ideas from without. No one is required to undergo any tremendous intellectual exertions. . . . Instead of a star, [the country man] hitches his wagon to the placid family mule and feels very virtuous and deserving if he can attain a comfortable dog trot. [Young, p. 77]

However seriously Ransom wished to be taken here, he hints at an emerging dualism—though not yet the careful "Body-Soul," "Reason-Emotion" formulations of his later thought—an early instance of intellect pulling against feelings. Whatever Ransom really believed about the rural South, the matter was settled during the summer of 1914, when unexpectedly he was offered a teaching position in Vanderbilt's English Department. In the areas of aesthetics, philosophy, morality, and art, his debating years were only beginning, and his ambivalent feelings about rural and urban life were soon to emerge in the debates that were his first poems. Given his rural background and intellectual tendencies, it is not surprising that Ransom would be drawn toward the use of some aspect of pastoral, a literary mode whose very center involves a contrast between a simple rural world and a complex, sophisticated world.

In this study, I try to show that Ransom's attitude toward his region and its values is ambiguous and that he uses *Poems About God,* his first volume, as a forum for discovering how he feels. I suggest that the persona is a college-trained young man from a rural community who quarrels with his father and God about moral values; that the pastoral forms he uses are negative ones, not unsuited to the polemical character of his thinking; and that the pastoral forms of his later poetry are subtler and more effective.

II

At the risk of oversimplification, I will glance now at a few aspects of the pastoral mode in an effort to show Ransom's connection with the tradition. Modern pastoral differs from classical pastoral in its avoidance, or alteration, of the conventions of the earlier form: greensward dances, the oaten pipe, the fair shepherdess and unhappy swain, singing contests, lengthy dialogues beneath the tree's shade, and Nature in active harmony with man—to mention several prominent ones. The spirit that underlay the older pastoral, however, was retained—the impulse to go back in time and place to a remembered innocence, the nostalgic backward glance to times when life was uncomplicated or to natural locales that were uncorrupted.

In our time, the term "pastoral" has come to refer to almost any literature which juxtaposes the complexities of urban life with the simplicities of a life removed—usually in rural surroundings, but not always. In modern pastoral, both Shepherd and Garden have undergone significant alteration. Shepherds are not always adult figures, though they are usually simple creatures—children or even animals. William Empson says that pastoral can embrace figures as disparate as Eve in the Garden and Alice in Wonderland. The Garden, too, is not confined to the "fresh woods and pastures new" of older pastorals, but could be any place of isolation or seclusion, even a room, from which a bucolic vision can be contemplated.

Yet some modern pastorals are truer to the older forms in their adherence to Gardenlike settings, presided over by shepherdlike individuals whose seemingly simple utterances nevertheless achieve a measure of profundity by dint of the speaker's double vision, or town-country perspective. John F. Lynen, for example, finds in Robert Frost's New England countryside and in his persona of the Yankee Farmer a pastoral structure with links to some of the *Idylls* of Theocritus. But what makes Frost's Arcadia particularly effective is its unity and stability; it is, as Lynen says, "a world, coherent and complete in itself."[3] And of particular importance in Frost's pastoral is the organic connection between the persona, the New England characters described in the poems, and the New England landscape itself. These three elements, plus the structure of the poetry, define Frost's pastoral.

Though there is a dim pastoral world visible in *Poems About God* and in Ransom's persona of an angry young man questioning the value system of his rural heritage, Ransom's Garden, Shepherd, and poetic structure do not yield the wholeness and coherence that Lynen finds in Frost's pastoral stance. The principal reason for this lack of an affirmative pastoral in Ransom is the frequently querulous tone of the speaker and an irony often affected for its own sake. Such an approach appears to fit Renato Poggioli's idea of an "inverted pastoral": "When self-conscious, the modern pastoral is, however, ironic and ambiguous, since it begins as imitation, and ends as parody. In brief, it is an inverted pastoral, presenting a bucolic aspiration only to deny it."[4] In *Poems About God*, we find instances of Ransom using the ironic and ambiguous inverted pastoral, wherein he establishes a bucolic hope or possibility and then negates it. This form is particularly well suited to the poet's questioning and ambiguous state of mind as he considers his inherited values from rural Tennessee and his sophisticated learning from the world beyond. And not only does he employ this ironic form, which inclines toward the negative, but also another form which inclines even further from the pastoral yearning—the anti-pastoral which militates against the idyllic assumptions of pastoral. As one critic describes this form, the Mower undermines Nature by being a "Mower *against* Gardens."[5] In time, Ransom returns to less negative pastoral forms, as I will show later, and particularly to a form of mock-pastoral which effectively burlesques some of the conventions of older pastorals; but next I will illustrate versions of his earliest use of the inverted pastoral.

III

In *Poems About God*, the inverted pastoral is found generally in two kinds of structures: either within lines of those poems not otherwise concerned with pastoral matters, or within stanzas or larger units of those poems with pastoral concerns. A good example of the first is "Under the Locusts," a poem of seven stanzas, each a random vignette of life spoken by one old man to other old men as they discourse idly in the shade of locust trees. Note in the two stanzas below how an idyll is sketchily proposed in the first two lines but negated in the next two:

Dick's a sturdy little lad
Yonder throwing stones;
Agues and rheumatic pains
Will fiddle on his bones.
....
Jenny and Will go arm in arm.
He's a lucky fellow;
Jenny's cheeks are pink as rose,
Her mother's cheeks are yellow.[6]

Of more moment to us here, however, are the inverted pastoral elements found within the structures of poems with predominantly pastoral concerns. I will mention two, though there are a number of others that would serve as well. "The Ingrate" begins with a description of a bucolic idyll: a rural Tennessee farm at night, the tasseled corn illumined by a golden moon. Entranced by the sight, the speaker praises the loveliness of the Garden to his visiting Russian friend, anticipating a similar response. But the Russian reacts in a jeering way, angering the speaker and thereby negating the bucolic hope. If the episode could be thought of as a kind of "singing" contest between the two "shepherds," the conclusion is not peaceful but ironic, the title of the poem serving as the speaker's (heavy-handed) judgment of his Russian friend. The idyll seems to have been established in order to be denied, and the main focus of the poem is on the speaker's frustration.

Another inverted pastoral is "Grace," which could have been subtitled "The Death of the Hired Man." The poem begins with a bucolic picture of two men working together on a farm—the speaker and the hired man. They are shown plowing together, singing together, talking religion amiably, and eating together at the speaker's mother's dinner table, savoring her country cooking. After dinner, they smoke their pipes and return to their plowing. Without warning, the idyll is shattered when the hired man slumps to the furrow, ill and dying. The speaker, dazed and uncomprehending, drags his friend to the shade, where both men regurgitate their meals and where the hired man dies, while the speaker denounces God for permitting this senseless death. At the conclusion of the poem, Nature participates in the action, not sympathetically as in the older pastorals, but ironically:

The little clouds came Sunday-dressed
To do a holy reverence,
The young corn smelled its sweetest too,
And made him goodly frankincense,
The thrushes offered music up,
Choired in the wood beyond the fence.
And while his praises filled the earth
A solitary crow sailed by,
And while the whole creation sang
He cawed—not knowing how to sigh. [pp. 22–23]

The solitary crow prefigures Ransom's later use of animals to provide ironic commentaries on the doings of men: "Necrological" and "Captain Carpenter," for example. If the poet here presents a bucolic idyll, he ruptures it by denouncing God and by questioning God's ways. As a matter of fact, this denunciation represents the expulsion of God from his own Garden, rendering the poem very nearly anti-pastoral.

Indeed, in this volume there are poems in which the tone hovers between inverted and anti-pastoral, one poem "The School" beginning with an anti-pastoral stance, but reversing itself near the end. In this poem the speaker considers the opposing claims of his classical education abroad and his rural Tennessee heritage. Stanza two establishes an anti-pastoral view:

Equipped with Grecian thoughts, how could I live
Among my father's folk. My father's house
Was narrow and his fields were nauseous,
I kicked the clods for being common dirt. [p.72]

But at the end of the poem, the speaker reverses this position; and because of the intercession of a benign diety ("The Lord preserves his saints for Christian uses"), he will deny and forget those "dead Greek empires" and return to his rural heritage. The "conversion" is less convincing here than the speaker's anger with his Maker in other poems.

Another poem with anti-pastoral features is "One Who Rejected Christ," which bears a striking resemblance to Frost's early poem "The Tuft of Flowers." Frost's poem concerns a farmer plowing ground that his neighbor had earlier mowed, and his discovery that the mower had spared a tuft of flowers from the scythe—for no other reason than "sheer morning gladness" in him. The experience gladdens the heart of the farmer, assuring him that even when men are apart, they work together. In the poem, the bucolic idyll is established, briefly threatened when the farmer senses the loneliness of his work, but triumphantly (if sentimentally) affirmed at the end. Ransom's version works in opposite ways.

In "One Who Rejected Christ," the speaker, a braggart, boasts of his unique ability to obtain more yield from an acre of land than his neighbors can, because unlike them, he plows up unprofitable plants, such as roses:

> A very good thing for farmers
> If they would learn my way:
> For crops are all that a good field grows,
> And nothing is worse than a sniff of rose
> In the good strong smell of hay. [p.17]

If the Machine here mows the Garden with a vengeance, we must remember that this particular speaker has been invented to say the opposite of what is meant (the title of the poem consigning the villain to an anti-heaven). The sense of the poem, of course, is close to what Frost was saying: aesthetic contemplation has an important place in our economic lives. To transmit this sentiment, Ransom uses a negative or inverted stance, while Frost's approach is direct and affirmative. Therein lies an important distinction between the two poets' earliest pastoral stances, which is not to say that Frost makes no use of negative features in his pastorals.

As a matter of fact, negative occurrences are by no means forbidden in the pastoral mode, and Frost (early and late) uses them in abundance. Generally, however, if he introduces an unexpectedly tragic event, he tends to weave it subtly into the fabric of his poem. Take, for example, one of his later anthology pieces " 'Out, Out—' " which seems to possess the principal ingredients for inverted pastoral. In the beginning, the poem establishes a bucolic idyll: a farmyard in which members of a family are completing the day's work and anticipating dinner, their young son hurrying to finish cutting wood with a buzz saw. The idyll is then abruptly denied: the buzz saw severs the boy's hand. But the poem is not inverted pastoral. The buzz saw is not introduced as an ironic device to thwart the bucolic hope, but rather to reveal the nature of the people and their way of life. As Lynen shows, there is an organic connection between the buzz saw, the boy's hand, and the need for "hands" to do farm work. From the beginning of the poem, the saw is present and is a normal adjunct to the work of the farm. Under the conditions of the poeple's coherent way of life, what happens is both inevitable and "normal." When the boy dies, the people do not quarrel with God about the injustice of that death; they turn stoically to their own affairs, grieving in their own way, but continuing the work of "hands" on the land.[7]

There is no reason, of course, why Ransom's early pastoral stance or his persona should be like Frost's—and every reason why it could not be: Frost was not a Methodist minister's son; did not grow up in the rural southern Bible Belt; had not undergone an exhaustive classical education here and abroad; and did not begin his writing under the shadow, so to speak, of a fundamentalist religious system. Rubin says that *Poems About God* shows "how unwilling Ransom was, despite his philosophical bent and his voyaging far from the orthodox Protestantism of his Methodist background, to give up the traditional religious attitude" [p.17]. Give it up he could not, but challenge it he could and did, using *Poems About God* as his forum for debate. As a forum and *form*, poetry offered Ransom a way of debating which provided more flexibility and indirectness than oral debate allowed, and the use of a persona spared him the possible embarrassment of contending directly with those he might offend. I believe that Ransom needed to understand rationally some of the connections between religion, region, and himself as artist before he felt capable of proceeding further into poetry and philosophy. And his poetic strategy for accomplishing this was to use, time and again, the persona of a young man from the country—perhaps a minister's son—whose recent advanced education prompts him to take issue with some of his parents' teachings.

The poems in this early volume are weaker than Frost's earliest poems, largely because Ransom appears to have valued content more than form; prose sense more than poetic detail; or, to use his later critical terminology, "structure" more than "texture." If many of his first poems are clumsy and inept, it should be noted that his whole poetic perspective at the time was a limited one, dictated largely by his need to explore a relatively narrow group of ideas and feelings associated with his father's values. After this volume, as we know, his subject matter broadened, his style became more complex, his persona matured, and structure and texture worked in closer concert. But first he had to quarrel with God, with his father, and with the value system he inherited. To put the matter metaphorically, before Ransom could contend with the larger community of art and ideas, he had to exorcise the ghosts of his rural heritage (ghosts with whom he later learned to live amiably).

IV

From inverted pastoral to a calmer, more philosophical pastoral, Ransom's development was dramatic, parallel in its swiftness to what Allen Tate said of the poet's general development after *Poems About God:* "overnight he had left behind him the style of his first book and without confusion had mastered a new style."[8] For example, the respected anthology piece "Bells for John Whiteside's Daughter" is not only one of Ransom's most nearly perfect lyrics but also his most effective pastoral, largely because of its country-town perspective, articulated with simplicity and wit by a mature, philosophical persona.

"Bells" concerns the death of a vivacious child whose energy and presence were so well defined in the neighborhood that the fact of her death is beyond the comprehension of the speaker and mourners. The locale of the poem is the country. The speaker appears to be a member of the community ("But now go the bells, and we are ready"), but he is also aware of how a more sophisticated outer world might react to this death—that is, of how such a world might appreciate subtle euphemism or refined language over simple rural language and clichés. The language of the poem reflects this double concern. Within the simplicity of diction throughout the poem there occur words of a more complex nature: the child is not said to be dead, but in a "brown study"; the mourners are not saddened, but "astonished" and "vexed," two words that not only serve to control a possible excess of sentiment, but also to elevate the experience to more complex levels. Moreover, the use of animals in a more conventionally pastoral sense—having the geese (the child's playmates) cry "in goose, Alas"—is a touch that would appeal both to the unsophisticated, such as children, and to the educated, who would not only sense the gentle irony of "Alas," but would recognize also the appropriateness of the pathetic fallacy in this context. This is no inverted pastoral. In the midst of our sadness over the child's death, we are made to yearn for the coherent and simple world of which she was a part.

Other pastorals of childhood that are similarly well made are "Blue Girls," "Janet Waking," "Dead Boy," "Vision by Sweetwater," and "First Travels of Max," but I will look at only one more of these. "Janet Waking" might seem to qualify as an inverted pastoral, since it begins with a bucolic aspiration—a young girl waking in anticipation of playing with her pet hen, and the denial of that hope when she discovers that Old Chucky has died. The poem, however, is not inverted pastoral. Its purpose is not to negate ironically the bucolic idyll, but to reveal Janet's inability to perceive the ironic and often humorous aspect of death, along with its terrible finality. Once again we have the juxtaposition of the child's simple world and the adult's complex, knowing world. The language of the poem points up these contrasts; for while the diction is simple at the beginning and end, it is erudite and sophisticated near the middle. For example, what killed Chucky was "a transmogrifying bee" that "sat" and "put the poison," and this action had the curious effect of causing Chucky's "poor comb" to stand up straight, while Chucky "did not." Despite the levity here (and pun on "not"), the speaker shows a fatherly sympathy for and understanding of Janet's grief. And through his awareness of how children and adults respond to a pet hen's death, we participate in a universally poignant moment.

Although Ransom wrote several other poems with pastoral features, I will conclude by examining at some length his work with a form of pastoral that is particularly well suited to his mature temperament—the mock-pastoral, as seen in the poem "Dog."[9] This clever poem, with its mock-heroic overtones and sophisticated and homely language, makes fun of the cliché, "A dog is man's best friend." The narrative element, delayed until stanza four, is preceded by twelve seemingly unrelated lines that serve as its prelude. Within these lines the speaker characterizes his Garden-World by describing the various voices of its inhabitants: the brass-lined rooster's "Cocka-doodle-doo", the fat Greek frog's "Brekekekex", and the dog's "Bow-wow-wow."

Noting that the sound of a dog bothers him more than other sounds, the speaker nevertheless confesses that he once "had a doggie who used to sit and beg." The familiar and expected second line of the nursery rhyme, "But doggie tumbled down the stairs and broke his little leg," is, however, withheld, prompting the reader to prepare himself for parody. The speaker continues by saying that his "Huendchen" was both housebroken and wise, not at all like the big dogs with their "fireman's bell" voices, nor like Fido, the dainty lap-dog, who recites his "pink paradigm, To yap." Thus, in the Garden live wise dogs, noisy dogs, and petite dogs, along with roosters, frogs, and people whose passion for their doggies is beyond belief.

Having established a tenuous connection between the prelude and the rest of the poem (texture cleverly overpowers structure in "Dog"), the speaker is now ready to begin the narrative. We watch the progress of a "tender bull" who rushes up the lane in amorous pursuit of his "twenty blameless ladies of the mead," who adore him and encourage his attentions. But the bucolic idyll is denied when the bull encounters fierce oppostion from a belligerent dog who, seemingly out of pure malice, sets up a barking that counters the bull's advance. Furious and threatening violence, the bull attacks the dog, but succeeds only in doing injury to the Garden, his hooves slicing the claybank and slashing the green vines, and his horn shredding the young birch into splinters. But the "bitch's boy" is unscathed. Finally, on the horizon appears Hodge, master of the Garden, who comes forward, cudgel in hand and blue eyes aflame, to whip the dog to kennel. Though temporarily defeated, the glowering dog apparently plots to disrupt again the idyllic atmosphere of the Garden.

The battle between canine and bovines is at once mock-pastoral and mock-heroic, since it involves a brave but ineffectual bull who strives to uphold the honor of his "blameless ladies" against a formidable enemy. In Arcadia, as we know, animals and insects were used as vocalists and/or instrumentalists, often providing an encouraging accompaniment to human discourse. Ransom's Garden resounds with a cacophony of animal chorus, some of it a prelude to the actual battle, but most of it a part of the fierce encounter.

Ransom has orchestrated his piece carefully. We hear first the tentative sounds of rooster and frog, followed by a kind of *leitmotif*—a dog's bow-wow, which is repeated with variations by Huendchen, Loud Dog, and finally Lap Dog. The overture completed, we hear the "hateful barking" of Hodge's dog, followed by the bellowing of the frustrated bull; and this sound is counterpointed by the "sorrowing moo" of the cows. And finally Hodge (whose name in English literature carries pastoral associations) comes forward angrily with his own vocal (and anti-pastoral) response, and harrows his dog to kennel and to silence.

Thus, the Garden in Ransom's "Dog" teems with animal speech, the carefully wrought, ornate language of the poem—with its genial blending of the colloquial and classical—inviting an allegorical reading. The sounds of the Garden almost certainly signify the absurdity of all utterance; and the fury accompanying the sound must surely point to the folly of all human endeavor. Beyond this, Ransom seems to have burlesqued other matters of genuine concern to him: his rural heritage, his classical training, and his love of argument and discourse.

If I have commented at length on a poem that has elicited little attention and less praise, it is because in the context of this essay, "Dog" is perhaps Ransom's most mature poem—mature in that he was able here to confront satirically (not polemically) both his rural background and his sophisticated training, place these influences within a pastoral framework, and treat them without rancor or reverence, but with genial wit and irony.

Poggioli said that modern pastoral begins as "imitation and ends as parody." Perhaps "Dog" was Ransom's farewell to pastoral and maybe even to poetry itself; for by the end of 1925, when the poem was published, he had written his best poems. In a few more years, he would engage strenuously in the Agrarian debates, siding, of course, with the Agrarians against their Industrialist opponents. Tiring of this contention, he eventually would move to a new vantage point geographically and intellectually, where, at Kenyon College in Ohio, he would spend the rest of his life debating critical theory with local and international friends and opponents.

A restless man who thrived on new ideas and vantage points, John Crowe Ransom was not a pastoralist of substantial dimensions, like Robert Frost. He wrote neat clusters of poems of various pastoral persuasion, just as he wrote clusters of romantic, satiric, and metaphysical poems. However much he understood the pastoral mode when he began writing poetry (his later criticism of "Lycidas" is another matter), he was undoubtedly affected by the joint impact of his rural upbringing and his classical education, traits which often conspire in the production of pastoral literature.

What we can say with certainty is that the pastoral tincture was present early and late in his poetry, and it provided a base or vantage point for the writing of some of his best verse. If his love for abstract thought and his awareness of the values of urban life are well documented, so are his love for the country and for "the common actuals." And these twin loves finally merged amiably in the dialectic that was his poetry.

Notes

This essay, in slightly altered form, was presented at the annual convention of the South Atlantic Modern Language Association in Atlanta, Georgia, on 12 November 1982.

1. *Gentleman in a Dustcoat* (Baton Rouge: Louisiana State University Press, 1976), p. 17.
2. *The Wary Fugitives* (Baton Rouge: Louisiana State University Press, 1978), p. 63.
3. *The Pastoral Art of Robert Frost* (New Haven: Yale University Press, 1960), p. 155.
4. "The Oaten Flute," *Harvard Library Bulletin* 11 (Spring 1957): 177.
5. Harold E. Toliver, "Marvell's Pastoral Vision," in *Pastoral and Romance*, ed. Eleanor Terry Lincoln (Englewood Cliffs, New Jersey: Prentice-Hall, 1969), p. 140.
6. *Poems About God* (New York: Holt, 1919), p. 38.
7. Lynen, 21–36.
8. Quoted in Young, 105.
9. *Selected Poems* (New York: Knopf, 1974), pp. 52–53.

Philip Castille

East Toward Home: Will Percy's Old World Vision

William Alexander Percy wrote his autobiography in Greenville, Mississippi, during the bad years of the Depression and the onset of World War II. During its composition, his health failed and he knew he was dying. His sole prose work, *Lanterns on the Levee: Recollections of a Planter's Son* was published by Knopf in 1941, shortly before Percy's death. Somewhat surprisingly, given the somber circumstances of its inception and preparation, the book is best remembered for its charming and wistful view of the bygone plantation world of the Mississippi Delta. Always a steady seller and now available in paperback reprint, *Lanterns on the Levee* remains today one of the South's favorite books.

However, despite the attention paid to southern manners in *Lanterns on the Levee,* Percy's intentions are more ideological than regional. The real strength of this autobiography lies not, as has often been claimed, in its pastoral treatment of the South. Unlike the Vanderbilt Agrarians, Percy writes less to celebrate the land than to eulogize the landowning class and the hierarchic society founded upon ownership of land, as in Europe. Percy extols the preindustrial civilization of the southern planter class only to insist that its extinction is but part of a larger destruction of Old World culture. Similarly, he decries the mass psychic impoverishment of contemporary urban life and solemnly predicts a new industrial Dark Age.

But, despite his misgivings, Percy does not counsel despair or cynicism. The active intent of Percy's autobiography is to guide his spiritual heirs toward moral and social commitment. While the prevailing mood of *Lanterns on the Levee* is regret for the overthrow of the ideals and authority of the southern plantocracy, its practical purpose is to use the remembered past to dispel the modernist sentiment that life has no meaning. Percy invokes the entire western cultural heritage both to assert the possibility of a good life founded on a firm sense of humane values and to encourage adherence to traditional standards of courage and dignity.

In Percy's vision, the Old World cultural tradition, sprung from biblical and classical roots, had crossed the Atlantic and flourished in the Old South in general and in Greenville, Mississippi, in particular. It had survived the military defeat of the Civil War and extended into the postbellum era of his father. By linking his little Delta town with such ancient cultural sources, Percy commits himself to a vision of historical continuity in which "General Lee and Senator Lamar would have been at ease, even simpatico, with Pericles and Brutus and Sir Philip Sidney."[1] While such a claim risks tendentiousness, it is not idle:

> The South—as well as other American colonies founded by Spain, Portugal, and France—was socially a scion of the seigneurial class of Europe. Ideologically it was a scion of the Italian Renaissance; and, as England was under the spell of such culture more than Spain or Portugal, this was truer of the English Southern colonies than of the Latin-American colonies.[2]

When Percy, whose paternal line had its origins in Northumberland, compared southern planters to Old World models, he was in full earnest. To be sure, Will Percy's patrician qualities were often attested to, notably in character sketches by David Cohn, Hodding Carter, and Jonathan Daniels. And even a southern skeptic like W. J. Cash was impressed enough to write, "Percy is that exceedingly rare thing, a surviving authentic Southern aristocrat, as distinguished from pretenders to the title."[3] But more impressively, a fineness of spirit shines through *Lanterns on the Levee*; and while it may be "impossible to convey to anyone who did not know him the peculiar charm and uniqueness of his gifts . . . the tone of *Lanterns on the Levee* comes as close as the written word can."[4]

The structure of Percy's autobiography falls into three sections, unified by the developing personality of the author. The first twelve chapters are given over to background and schooling, the effort of the child and youth to learn the traditional values and standards of Old World culture. In the middle section (Chapters XIII-XXIII), Percy recounts his effort as a young man to confront the twentieth-century issues of war, race, and economics and to live up to the example of his distinguished father. In the closing section (Chapters XXIV-XXVIII), he describes his attempt to be a father and instruct his adopted sons, as he had been instructed, in the tenets of the classically-minded, hierarchical plantation world of the Old South.

Although he does not "enter" the book until Chapter III, Percy imprints his stamp on the two introductory chapters. He describes the geographical locus of the book, the Mississippi Delta, and the origins of its dynastic culture. But, while evoking the spirit of the past, he keeps a firm rein on the imposing reality of the present, "a new order unsure of itself and without graciousness" [p. 9]. Contemporary instability is set off against the abiding presence of the river, which figures throughout as a symbol of eternity. Under mounting pressure from American mass society, the old agrarian hierarchy is tottering. "Behind us a culture lies dying," he laments, "before us the forces of the unknown industrial world gather for catastrophe" [p. 24]. Among the victims of this onslaught will be his father, Senator LeRoy Percy, in whom Will Percy saw the embodiment of the Old World tradition of personal probity and public responsibility.[5] The sociodrama that his father lived through and that Will Percy (born in 1885) inherited is the defeat of the southern plantocracy, not by the Civil War, but by a new urban-industrial class, ignorant of its cultural past, "poor in spirit and common as hell" [p. 62]. Before its tide, not only is the southern tradition helpless, but also the entire cultural tradition of western civilization: "Under the Southern Valhalla the torch has been thrust, already the bastions have fallen. . . . A side-show Götterdämmerung perhaps, yet who shall inherit our earth, the earth we loved?" [p. 63]. Percy's insistence here, and throughout the book, is on the large-scale implications of the collapse of southern plantation civilization: the southern apocalypse provides but local testimony to the global disappearance of the landholding class and its aristocratic institutions.

Looking backward from the aspect of maturity, it thus appeared to Percy that the underlying principle of his life had been his "doomed" vocation as a planter's son, the descendant of a classical, agrarian Old World tradition now almost extinguished. But as a boy and young man, he did not perceive himself or his mission as such. Chapters VIII-XII recount his student years and ambitions. He graduated in 1904 from the University of the South at Sewanee, Tennessee, where he later taught English. He studied at the Sorbonne and in 1908 received his law degree from Harvard. In Chapter XII he touches upon his "first" career—not as a planter's son but as a poet. During his lifetime, four volumes of poetry were printed: *Sappho in Levkas* (1915), *In April Once* (1920), *Enzio's Kingdom* (1924), and *Selected Poems* (1930). Also, he served as editor of the Yale Series of Younger Poets, in 1923 and 1925 and from 1927 to 1931.[6] However, after 1924, Percy turned away from writing poetry to assume the public responsibilities of his hometown and the Delta. Although briefly describing this literary aspect of his life, Percy states flatly that *Lanterns on the Levee* "is not an account of my poetry nor of me as a poet" [p. 131]. With this declaration, Percy effectively closes the first section of his autobiography.

In the middle section of the book (Chapters XIII-XXIII), Percy records the crises of adult life and his effort to measure up to the standards of the past. In a pivotal chapter, "The Bottom Rail on Top" (XIII), he recounts his father's resounding defeat in 1912, losing his Senate seat. His victorious opponent was James K. Vardaman, who was nicknamed "Great White Father" for his racist policies. Vardaman was joined in the fight by Theodore G. Bilbo, another folk hero who in 1911 narrowly had escaped expulsion from the state senate on bribery charges. Percy saw his father voted out by "the sort of people that lynch Negroes, that mistake hoodlumism for wit, and cunning for intelligence, that attend revivals and fight and fornicate in the bushes afterwards" [p. 149]. His father's crushing defeat was the turning point of Will Percy's life, for it presaged the disintegration of the plantation way of life. Further, Percy foresaw that the displacement of the southern plantocracy was cause for far more than regional alarm: "today Mississippi is like the rest of the South and the South is like the rest of the nation. . . . The voters choose their representatives in public life, not for their wisdom or courage, but for the promises they make" [p. 153]. While Vardaman might seem only a backwater menace, to Percy he was an ominous forerunner of a new breed of cultural barbarians whose rise signalled the collapse of humanism, not only in America but also in Europe:

> In Russia, Germany, and Italy Demos, having slain its aristocrats and intellectuals and realizing its own incompetence to guide or protect itself, had submitted to tyrants who laughed at the security virtues and practiced the most vile of the survival virtues with gangster cynicism. In the democracies Demos had been so busy providing itself with leisure and luxury it had forgotten that hardihood and discipline are not ornaments but weapons. [p. 312]

The onset of World War I confirmed Percy's suspicions that humanism was dying not only in Mississippi and America but the world over. Unable to live in the lost world and unwilling to live in the new one, Percy somewhat to his astonishment found grateful relief from his alienation in the common cause of the war. His years of soldiering (Chapters XIV-XVII) were, by his own admission, the only time in his life when he had any fun. Also, he distinguished himself in action in northeastern France and was awarded the Croix de Guerre in 1918. But in 1919, returning to Greenville and its heritage of defeat, his pessimism for the twentieth century was renewed by the rebirth of the Ku Klux Klan (Chapter XVIII). "The most poisonous thing the Klan did to our town," he recalls, "was to rob its citizens of their faith and trust in one another. . . . from Klansmen you could expect neither frankness nor truth nor honor, and you couldn't tell who was a Klansman" [p. 237]. The fragmentation of Greenville seemed total, neighbor against neighbor in an ugly atmosphere of suspicion and violence. Years of rancor followed until, suddenly, in 1927 planters and river-rats, Catholics and Klansmen, blacks and poor whites were united in disaster by the great Mississippi flood (Chapter XIX). Joined in common subjection to the river, invoked earlier as the presiding deity of the Delta, these diverse elements once again came together in an order resembling that fostered by the old plantocracy. Percy himself served as state chairman of the Disaster Relief Committee of the Red Cross. But this enforced return to the old ways of getting along with one another was short lived; enmity and mistrust soon reasserted themselves. Percy's point is clear: the old planter kingdom is in disarray, and not even the mighty river can restore it.

Chapter XX and the three that follow present Percy's effort to vindicate himself and the tradition by which he has lived from "Northern liberal" criticism. In "Planters, Share-Croppers, and Such" (XXI), he marshals facts and statistics to explain to an industrial world an outdated agricultural system. Percy's voice turns uncharacteristically tinny in this vain effort, lashing out at "Knights of the Bleeding Heart" while disclosing little about why the southern economy has done badly in relation to northern urban-industrialism. However, in "Fode" (XXII), he writes movingly of the plight of his chauffeur and tries to depict the appeal and tragedy of southern blacks. Percy cuts through the abstractions and rhetoric to present concretely the human aspect of the problem and its great measure of personal involvement. Ford is a reality, not a theory, and Percy admits there are no easy answers to the problems of race and economics, and perhaps no way out at all. In Chapter XXIII, he makes his uncertainty explicit: "It is true in the South that whites and blacks live side by side, exchange affection liberally, and believe they have an innate and miraculous understanding of one another. But the sober fact is we understand one another not at all" [p. 299]. Ending on this plaintive note, Percy implies that blacks will fare no better, and perhaps far worse, in the urban ghettoes of the industrial North (and New South) than they did on the plantations of the Old South.[7]

These observations close the middle section of the book, eleven chapters devoted to Percy's attempts to confront the issues of adult life in the spirit of his father and in the tradition of the landowning class. With the death of Senator Percy in 1929, Will Percy assumed responsibility for running Trail Lake, the family plantation, and seemed to be confirmed in lifelong bachelorhood. However, two years later he found himself responsible for rearing three young cousins, orphaned by the deaths of their parents. He sensed a profound alteration in a life already settled into middle age. "Just as his maturity had begun when he learned from the past generation," writes Lewis Lawson, "so now he is obligated to become the past generation for his sons and provide them with the philosophy that will insure their successful maturity."[8]

Percy's effort to hand down the planter ideal begins in "For the

Younger Generation" (Chapter XXIV), in which *Lanterns on the Levee* reaches its climax. Faced with educating his young charges, Percy is driven to a defense of the precepts by which he has lived. But in so doing, he must wrestle with the issue of whether his teachings are adequate in the modern world. Should he teach them an Old World creed which he still holds but which he suspects has been superannuated, or should he

> teach deceit, dishonor, ruthlessness, bestial force to the children in order that they survive? Better that they should perish. It is sophistry to speak of two sets of virtues, there is but one: virtue is an end in itself. . . . Honor and honesty, compassion and truth are good even if they kill you, for they alone give life its dignity and worth. [p. 313]

The values and ideals of the spiritual good life remain, and the culture of preindustrial western civilization abides even in the modern world. Classical in its origins and humanistic in its values, Percy's Old World vision is both the mainspring of *Lanterns on the Levee* and its legacy: "there is but one good life and men will yearn for it and will again practice it. . . . Love and compassion, beauty and innocence will return. It is better to have breathed them an instant than to have supported iniquity a millenium" [p. 313].

Though the bottom rail is everywhere on top, Old World ideals never die completely and never change at all. In brief, therein lies the theme of the book: standards of competence and courage that we measure ourselves by, and ideals of right thinking and clean living that we follow—these have not been improved upon by the present age. Only by recourse to the past—the cultural continuity of western civilization—can the deficiencies of our own time be exposed and perhaps, in the total picture, corrected. The passive, survivalist virtues count for very little; only an unswerving commitment to classical styles of bravery and beauty can give grace and meaning to life and lift it above brutality and confusion.

The concluding chapter of *Lanterns on the Levee,* "Home," is set in the Greenville cemetery, but its spiritual locus lies far away. On the last page of his autobiography, Percy's thoughts drift eastward from his "tiny outpost" [p. 347] in Mississippi. In this ultimate vision, an Old World fortress rises before him where godlike forms pace the ramparts. They do not look southern. Below them, Will Percy, having discharged his duty to the younger generation, cries for admission, seeking at last his spiritual "true" home.

More than forty years after its appearance, *Lanterns on the Levee* thus stands as something of an oddity. Perhaps readers will continue to find in it an idyllic portrayal of a vanished South, and some may link it to the Agrarian movement of the twenties and thirties. But Percy seems a doubtful southern chauvinist. Though his sense of civic commitment is strong (and he is careful to stress the importance of community), Percy's motivation in writing *Lanterns on the Levee* is only incidentally regional. From Greenville to Moscow, the land-holding class appeared doomed. At basis Percy is more concerned with the worldwide disappearance of hierarchic social structures than with fading images of the cotton kingdom, and more dedicated to the preservation of classical values than of sharecropping. Will Percy's main intention in his autobiography is to hand down to his descendants the heritage of a planter civilization whose antecedents stretched eastward toward the dynastic preindustrial culture of the Old World. By appreciating the frankly ideological nature of the book, we can come to understand better Will Percy's impassioned defense of his life, his homeland, and his class, and perhaps come more to admire his success in extending the tradition he memorializes.

Notes

This essay, in slightly altered form, was presented at the Annual Convention of the Modern Language Association in Los Angeles, California, on 28 December 1982.

1. *Lanterns on the Levee: Recollections of a Planter's Son* (1941; rpt. Baton Rouge: Louisiana State University Press, 1973), pp. 62–63.

2. Raimondo Luraghi, *The Rise and Fall of the Plantation South* (New York: New Viewpoints, 1978), p. 33. In this Marxist perspective, the southern planter, along with his Canadian, West Indian, Brazilian, and Latin American counterparts, is seen as the legitimate heir of a "seigneurial" Old World culture in sharp ideological opposition to mercantile and industrial capitalism.

3. Review of *Lanterns on the Levee* in *Charlotte News*, 10 May 1941, rpt.

in Joseph L. Morrison, *W. J. Cash: Southern Prophet* (New York: Knopf, 1967), p. 291.

4. Letter received from Walker Percy, 17 November 1971.

5. For a psychological examination of Will Percy's relationship with his father, see Richard H. King, "Mourning and Melancholia: Will Percy and the Southern Tradition," *Virginia Quarterly Review* 53 (Spring 1977): 248–264.

6. For an account of Percy's career as a poet, see Benjamin Willis Dickey, "William Alexander Percy: An Alien Spirit in the Twentieth Century," M.A. Thesis, Auburn University, 1951

7. The question of Percy's alleged paternalistic or racist attitude toward blacks after all may be moot. For a discussion of the complexities of the larger issue, see Eugene D. Genovese, "Class and Race," *The World the Slaveholders Made* (New York: Vintage, 1971), pp. 103–113.

8. "Walker Percy's Southern Stoic," *Southern Literary Journal* 3 (Fall 1970): 7.

Michael Kreyling

After the War: Romance and the Reconstruction of Southern Literature

The southern writer in the closing decades of the nineteenth century faced pressures at once more powerful, enticing, and subtle than had ever faced him in, for example, the furious years of the sectionalist crisis of the 1850s. *The* southern author of that decade, William Gilmore Simms, reacted to the pressure with fiction that served his polemical purpose: the demolition of Yankee prejudice and the veneration of southern mores and institutions.

Three writers of the postbellum decades, Lafcadio Hearn, Grace King, and George Washington Cable, encountered less overt pressures. They were persuaded—forced, cajoled, flattered—into producing a literature that aimed to capitalize on the extra-regional popularity of New Orleans and to serve several extra-literary purposes: the entertainment of a nonsouthern reading audience eager for the picturesque and exotic escape the South afforded; the confirmation, by eminent natives, of the moral victory of the War and Reconstruction; the outsider's identification of romance as the cultural "fingerprint" of the southern imagination. In some cases the pressure was as simple as a formula sent down from a northern editorial desk. More often it was a complex blend of personal ambition, a sense of literary competition, and a changing view of the interaction of literature with its cultural-political setting. In the three writers I have chosen we can find evidence of pressure to deal with southern materials in a certain way—to become, thereby, a certain type of southern writer.

Hearn: The Business of Southern Literature

Lafcadio Hearn (1850-1904), born on an island off the coast of Greece, raised by an Irish-Catholic great-aunt, educated by Jesuits in England and in France, trained in journalism at the scenes of grisly murders and other unsavory sights, is an unlikely candidate for the honor roll of southern writers. He only spent about eight and one-half years in the South (November 1878 to June 1887 in New Orleans, with a side trip to Florida) working on the New Orleans *Item* and *Times-Democrat*. He wrote southern sketches for *Harper's*, and capped his brief southern career with the novel *Chita* (1889). Hearn, however, could not have been in the South at a better time. He was present for most of Cable's career in the city, and for the beginning of King's revision of Cable's treatment of Creole civilization. He was on hand for the visits of Richard Watson Gilder and Charles Dudley Warner, and for the attention of Henry Mills Alden. In short, Hearn was on the scene for the making of southern literature, Creole style. He even made some of it himself.

But Hearn must always remain something of a Shreve character, always asking *why* people live in the South, never knowing in the blood as Quentin Compson knows. To Hearn, nourished on the literature of his beloved French romantics (Hugo, Gautier, Loti, deMaupassant) "South" meant Latin, Mediterranean, equatorial. The history, politics, social order and social dream of the American South were not his. Hearn never came close to knowing the South from within. He knew only those circumstantial things that publishers, readers, and some of his own friends were eager to have him produce. In Hearn's ambition to generate this literary product, and in statements that evidence his attitude toward the situation of the South and the southern writer's postbellum literary situation, we have one angle—the commercial—on the making of southern literature in this period.

Unlike many writers of his day—of any day—Lafcadio Hearn had an acute if sometimes paranoiac sense of the literary marketplace. Editors to him were agents or brokers for large audiences which they cultivated and exploited. They elevated writers who supplied the most useful raw material. This is not to say that Hearn liked this situation; in fact he barely tolerated it. But tolerate it he did; it was the real as he knew it. To his way of thinking, the southern writer and his or her product were commodities. Acceptance and prestige were not a matter of breaking Yankee prejudice; they were a matter of marketing procedure, persistence, and luck:

> The Eastern magazines [he writes in 1881] are largely supported by rings of writers through which it is not easy for a novice to break; or again, they are maintained by contributions especially commanded from writers of established reputation, who received orders for articles just as a tailor for a suit of clothes.[1]

A writer must endure until he can break into the charmed circle—either with a superior suit of clothes, or with a new fashion that is sure to start a vogue. Hearn saw Cable as the initiator of such a vogue for the picturesque and exotic Creole tale. Indeed, Hearn's desire to come to New Orleans in 1877—ostensibly to report the outcome of the 1876 presidential recount—might partially be due to his ambition to get in on this trend somewhere near the ground floor. In "The Scenes of Cable's Romances," which he published in the *Century* in 1882 with Cable's support, Hearn reveals that coming from

> gray northeastern mists into the tepid and orange-scented air of the South, my impressions of the city, drowsing under the violet and gold of a November morning, were oddly connected with memories of 'Jean-ah Poquelin.' That strange little tale had appeared previously in the *Century*; and its exotic picturesqueness had considerably influenced my anticipations of the Southern metropolis, and prepared me to idealize everything peculiar and semi-tropical that I might see.[2]

So determined was Hearn to capitalize on these "anticipations" that he sent his Cincinnati newspaper picturesque travel pieces in lieu of the political news he had been dispatched to report. He continued to produce such pieces for the New Orleans papers on which he worked. He gave them titles such as "The Glamour of New Orleans" and turned out numerous sketches of Creole court yards, Creole songs, Creole character types, and Creole recipes, all at a time when he was writing to friends in his letters that "the climate is so debilitating that even energetic *thought* is out of the question" and "after a few years in Louisiana, hard work becomes impossible. We are all lazy, enervated, compared with you Northerners."[3]

But Hearn was determined to make his work and hardships pay off. He seemed, in 1885, about to crack the ring as a southern writer, about to furnish *Harper's* with a "suit of clothes." He wrote to a friend: "The Harpers are giving me warm encouragement; but advise me to remain a fixture where I am. They say they are looking now to the South for literary work of a certain sort,—immense fields for observation remain here wholly untilled, and that they want active, living, opportune work of a fresh kind" [Bisland, 1:338].

By 1887 he could report (whether proudly or ironically is a tantalizing question): "I have become a contributor to the [*Harper's*] *Magazine*, and am going to have the honour of a short sketch of myself in it,—of course, in connection with the New Southern Literary Movement" [Bisland, 1:381]. Also in 1887 he sent Henry Mills Alden of *Harper's* the manuscript of *Chita*, his attempt to claim his proper share of the literary marketplace, and a work he called, oddly, "an attempt at a treatment of modern southern life" [Bisland, 1:405]. It is curious that he should describe *Chita* in these words, for there is little or nothing of the "modern southern life" of Hearn's day in it. There is an abundance of atmosphere, exotic word painting, and Hearn's pantheistic philosophy. Of slavery and emancipation, of sectionalism or politics there is nothing—only a brief reverie involving two characters in a Chancellorsville bivouac.

The "modern southern life" of his day was something that Hearn did not really know. In his review of *Dr. Sevier*, a novel in which Cable was moving in the direction of critical analysis of the modern southern predicament during and immediately after the War, Hearn chided his now distant friend for the political and realistic aspects of the book. Cable, Hearn said, should stick to the scene painting that had made *Old Creole Days* and *The Grandissimes* so popular. Voicing this opinion Hearn echoes Cable's northern editors, Richard Watson Gilder and Robert Underwood Johnson, who preferred the charming to the real.

In his column for the New Orleans *Times-Democrat* (15 April 1883) Hearn elaborated on his view of southern literature:

> The idea that Northern people—especially Northern critics—are a

> set of ravenous wild beasts, lying in wait for the Southern literary lamb and ready to devour him on sight, is all a mistake. The Northern critics and editors and publishers and readers may be too indifferent to the just claims of Southern authors—we think they are too indifferent—but there is no *virus* of diabolical malignity in this indifference. It is a mere matter of business after all, and must be met and overcome by practical business methods—not by sentimental indignation and appeals to sectional rivalry. [Ichikowa, 112–113]

To Hearn's commercial view an unreconstructed reader wrote back from Little Rock, "The Northern critic, or publisher, comes to a Southern article with an old belief that 'nothing good can come out of Nazareth.' The old time prejudice against the South as offering any promise still finds strong root in the Northern mind" [New Orleans *Times-Democrat*, 6 May 1883]. The correspondent pointed to "Northern antagonism" and "Southern indifference" as the twin hardships of the southern writer. In his rebuttal, Hearn reiterated his belief that there was no "aggressive and malignant character" in northern attitudes toward the southern writer. Northern writers of inferior merit are published "because they [writers of the South] are unknown or obscure. They have not yet obtained a reputation sufficient to make their *names* an available and bankable currency in the literary market" [Ichikowa, 118, 119]. Hearn's consistent usage of the financial metaphor leads us to the inescapable conclusion that he saw southern material in the post-1877 literary market as a sound investment, not as a deeply personal world of experience for fiction. Therefore, he did not have much difficulty supplying *Harper's* with its desires.

Soon after Henry Mills Alden's letter accepting *Chita* arrived in 1887, Hearn left New Orleans forever, off on the next leg of his lifelong odyssey. He went first to New York to polish the proofs of *Chita*, then to Martinique in the West Indies, more nearly the South of his global imagination, the natural home of the "nude, warm, savage, amorous Southern nature" that counterpoised the "vigorous" Teutonic North that had constructed western civilization [Bisland, 1:424, 423].

Hearn's global imagination was too vast to afford much meaning to the distinction between American North and South in the latter days of the nineteenth century. The experience of the sundering was not a part of his personal memory; he did not land on American shores until 1869. To him the controversy and tension—spoken and unspoken—were a mask for literary economics. He saw the powerful literary establishments of his time as what we would now call "vertically integrated" monopolies: starting with serials, they also controlled the publishing of books, and naturally acquired authors and kept them in "immense fields of observation" like foremen at a mine or a mill. Hearn saw nothing sinister in this. To him it was the world of literary business and he meant to survive in it. He did; not in a princely fashion, but he did survive. To Lafcadio Hearn the Professional Writer, the sparring between the southern writer and the outside (i.e. northern) world of readers, editors, and critics, was not his fight. He had fights, but this was not one of them. His dispassionate and idiosyncratic view of issues gripping southern literature after 1877, however, casts light not otherwise available. If we believe Hearn, and with proper caution we may, there was a southern literary consciousness characterized by fear and suspicion of being manipulated and thwarted by the outsiders; there was a northern establishment at least tacitly distributing formulas or patterns for "literature of a certain sort" to writers whom they retained in certain fields; there was a popular southern literary industry that was all "gush" and "floriated English" [Ichikowa, 43]; and there was a vogue for the picturesque, exotic, Creole-flavored tale and sketch—exclusive of politics—that could sell magazines and, to a modest extent, financially support a southern writer.

Grace King: The Saving Remnant

Grace Elizabeth King (1851–1932)—daughter of an established New Orleans family that had suffered at the hands of occupying Yankee soldiers—knew Lafcacio Hearn only as someone "writing editorials on French Literature for our *Times-Democrat*."[4] She moved in circles—the intelligentsia of old New Orleans, faculty of Newcomb College and of Tulane, visiting genteel dignitaries like Julia Ward Howe, Charles Dudley Warner, and Richard Watson Gilder—in which Hearn was seldom to be found. Her perspective on the reconstruction of southern literature is significantly different. With memories of stolen silver and plundered cellars, she was immensely more sensitive on the issue than Hearn. Her memories of her mother's tales of fleeing the family sugar plantation, her own vacations at Charles Gayarre's place across Lake Pontchartrain, her conviction that race relations in the Old South were characterized by a "love which in the end will destroy all differences in color,"[5] make Grace King the writer an important window on the literary situation after 1877. Unlike Hearn, she was emotionally devoted to the Old South and more than skeptical of the New. Unlike Cable, she has been termed a social historian in the Jamesian manner who was in actuality the idealizing romanticist of a bygone Creole New Orleans. Her response to the pressure to be southern was more emotional and idealistic than Hearn's. In King's dealings with editors, we witness the southerner as cultural prophet convinced of the superiority and redemptive merit of the lost society.

Grace King began her literary career after a well known challenge from Richard Watson Gilder. Gilder, the influential editor of the *Century* and (at that time) Cable's staunch publisher, was in New Orleans for the Cotton Centennial Exposition of 1884. King's appraisal of Cable was none too flattering: "He was a native of New Orleans and had been well treated by its people, and yet he stabbed the city in the back, as we felt, in a dastardly way to please the Northern press" [*Memories*, 60]. He had then fled North, and "took no part in our Exposition" [*Memories*, 51]. As significant as is her sense of outrage is Grace King's identification with the South and with New Orleans through the use of the collective pronouns. More possessive of the South than Hearn, and hence with more to lose should it be exploited, King felt the issues shaping its literature more keenly. And she entered the lists, upon Gilder's challenge to better Cable, as a champion of southern manner and morals.

Not content to "submit to Cable's libels in resignation," King wrote her first piece of Southern fiction, "Monsieur Motte," and sent it to Gilder. It was promptly returned. Through the intercession of her friend, Charles Dudley Warner, the story soon found a publisher, the *New Princeton Review*, a publication of Arnoldian leanings which was also receptive to Gilder's literary criticism. The new author was praised by William Dean Howells who compared her to Hawthorne and the "French masters of fiction."[6] So popular was "Monsieur Motte" that the editor sent King an order (suggestion?) for a sequel to be set on a plantation, since plantations were popular. She supplied the story "'On the Plantation' almost on order" [Bush, 15]. King herself described the sequel as a conventional love story capitalizing on the hardy popularity of the picturesque Old South. But she did not feel manipulated. She was smoothly introduced into the literary mill and seems not to have felt pinching or crunching. The "smiling aspects of life" were her truth, her realism.

An especially stiff challenge to King's literary integrity came early in the new century when George P. Brett of Macmillan publishers suggested that she write a romance of the Reconstruction. Thomas Nelson Page and Thomas Dixon had had recent popular successes in this vein. The "order" is clear. Hearn, for instance, would have recognized its commercial nature at once. Whether Grace King recognized it as such is not known, but she was troubled. At this point in her career she was afraid that she had used up all the arrows in her "little quiver." But Brett "showed me the goodness that lies at the heart of the publishing autocrat by encouraging me to go on, if necessary in another field, and suggested that the reconstruction period in the South had always seemed to him a picturesque setting for a story" [*Memories*, 234]. King answered in a tone she feared was bitter and resentful that she could recollect nothing romantic about that period. Much of what she remembers saying to Brett appeared later as introductory matter to *The Pleasant Ways of St. Médard*, the novel that eventually grew out of the autocrat's suggestion: "The fighting the Papas had done in the war was nothing to the fighting they did afterwards, for bread and meat; and the bitterness of their defeat there was sweetness compared to the bitterness that came afterwards. Bayonet in hand was easier to them than hat in hand."[7] King's picture of occupation is filled with insolent, ill-mannered and frequently drunk Yankees. Her Reconstruction novel did not turn out to be the picturesque romance that Brett and Macmillan had hoped for, but instead a novel depicting:

> a country given over to lawlessness, a people demoralized, swarming freed negroes, an insolent soldiery, ruin, wretchedness, and despair, no one knowing what to do or where to begin work again in the uncertainty of what the victorious government intended further as punishment for the defeated. [p. 16]

The novel itself seldom escapes the fragmentary nature of recollection. Vignettes alternate with editorial asides on the inferiority of the Yankees and the freed slaves. There is much lamenting of the bottom rail on top; there is a seasoning of "historical" fact always relating to unfair or ill-bred conduct on the part of the carpetbaggers and scalawags. The "good" blacks reject freedom, pleading their inferior natures. There is a thin thread of plot concerning the jeopardy and eventual rescue of the fortunes of the central family, a dispossessed planter-lawyer and his wife and daughters.

King, knowing her novel had too much harsh criticism of the idealistic and "official" view of Reconstruction, sent the manuscript to Macmillan "with a foreboding heart" [*Memories*, 236]. Back it came with a kind letter but a negative verdict. Brett's formula for a romance of the Reconstruction waited until 1936 when Macmillan published *Gone With the Wind*. His patience paid off to the tune of one million copies in the first six months.

Grace King had run up against Reconstruction in more than one way with *The Pleasant Ways of St. Médard*. The rejection by Macmillan (the novel was eventually published by Holt in 1916) was her first hard experience of the invisible fortress the southern writer had to climb. She had been let in by the main gate when she supplied the love plot for "On the Plantation." But there would be no such favor for a book that showed Reconstruction as an offense and a political catastrophe. She lamented her fate to Thomas Nelson Page, who represented to her the epitome of the southern gentleman of letters. His advice was hearty:

> 'I know, I know,' he said. 'That was the fault they found with one of my novels. And I had to remedy it to get it published. Now I'll tell you what to do; for I did it! Just rip the story open and insert a love story. It is the easiest thing to do in the world. Get a pretty girl and name her Jeanne, that name always takes! Make her fall in love with a Federal officer and your story will be printed at once! The publishers are right; the public wants love stories. Nothing easier than to write them. You do it! You can do it. Don't let your story fail.' [*Memories*, 378]

As so often happens, we do not have a tone of voice to accompany Page's recipe. But we do know that the advice came after it was too late for King to do anything with it. This conversation, King says, took place in the year of Page's death, 1922. From the 1880s up to the 1920s the recipe for southern romance still fascinated publishers. And it still remained the onus of every southern writer striving for success in the only literary game in town.

King's life as a southern woman of letters illustrates aspects of the literary situation not elucidated by Hearn's. As a southerner of the patrician class, Grace King had deep spiritual roots in the myth of the genteel Old South. In 1903 she wrote: "I think the Country owes it to the South that we have a standard of easy and luxurious living; that the millionaires of to-day are glad to follow. Every home, club house—I may say every association for refined social life is modeled on ideals furnished by the South—just as surely as we model our financial associations on ideals furnished by the North" [Bush, 387]. Although Grace King might have felt the term New South "obnoxious" in 1884, she gradually became a mainstay of the southern remnant that would redeem modern mercantile America from the horrors of its own prosperity. She makes the arguments as unblinkingly as any dyed-in-the-wood Grady-ite.

Whether she was aware of this situation, her writing was gradually trimmed to the pattern that northern editors preferred. Hearn would have seen this as simple literary market pressure, but King, comfortably ensconced as a southern woman of letters, does not seem to have felt the change. George Washington Cable, however, faced with the same pressures, found Page's peptalk very true and very difficult to evade. His fate as a southern writer is the most complex of the three.

Cable: The Art of Resistance

Edward King, whose scouting trip for literary talent in the South in the early 1870s discovered no writer better than Cable, wrote to his friend in 1874 after he had, with some difficulty, finally placed one of Cable's Creole stories: "Persevere and graduate to New York as soon as you can."[8] The primacy of New York, then and now, was an acknowledged fact in the publishing world. Cable acknowledged it. The popularity of his picturesque Creole tales had launched a vogue—had drawn Hearn to New Orleans, had roused King and her set—and had made his publishers a few dollars. Cable saw some of those dollars, and in the late 1870s while *Ole Creole Days* and the serialized *The Grandissimes* were strengthening his reputation, he became more serious about "graduating" to New York. He queried his editors about the possibilities of living by his pen in the North. But the more popular he grew as a southern writer, the more acutely he felt the vise of genteel literary politics. Hearn was never seriously caught in this particular vise, and to Grace King its embrace was velvet. For Cable, however there were scars.

The pattern of romance that Page heartily recommended to King was also pressed upon Cable by his editors. In response to Cable's letter about the possibility of moving to New York, Robert Underwood Johnson, Gilder's lieutenant at the *Century*, communicated the recipe:

> I wish I were able to write a novel. I'll tell you what I would do. The greatness of Lessing in German literature dates from his *Minna von Barnhelm*, the first German comedy (about 1750). Previously, Prussia and Saxony had been fighting and jealously deprecating each other. After the war, Lessing embodied in this beautiful play two types of character who did more for German unity than Bismarck himself! His hero was a manly Prussian—his heroine a refined Saxon, and he the mediator and conciliator between the two nations. *Minna* is today the most popular German comedy not excepting Goethe and Schiller.
>
> Well, the time is soon coming when this sort of a work must be done for us. As long as the conventional types of Yankee and Reb. are kept before the people, *i.e.* as long as politicians have axes to grind—so long will the reunion of the people be delayed. Had I the knowledge and the power, I would write a novel aiming to do this: hold up the best side of the South and North during the War of Secession. Here is romance ready made—no great writer—of *our great* writers of fiction—has touched the War. Northern politicians (and perhaps Southern ones) are teaching the youth of the South to hate the Union worse than their fathers. My novel should work against this current. Preaching and speech-making can do nothing. Fiction can do much. The present generation would read fiction of our war with avidity. Bret Harte once told me that he thought a great literature of fiction would come out of the war and that when it was written the pathos would be on the side of the invaded and desolated South. Have your plans ever extended in this direction?[9]

Johnson was to mention his recipe (political reconciliation through fictional romances) to Thomas Nelson Page a few years later.[10] Page came close to cornering the market and giving the form his name.

But Cable's difficulties in supplying this product illustrate much about the reconstruction of southern literature after the compromise of 1877.

Cable's next major fiction after he received this letter was the novel *Dr. Sevier*. Hearn, we have seen, found fault with the inclusion of politics. The reviewer for the *Atlantic Monthly* (January 1885) also thought the novel too much like a "tract." Gilder, who read the manuscript pages as Cable sent them up to him, tried to stifle this aspect of the novel. He liked the peripheral Creole characters for their colorful speech. He would even admit that the war scenes were powerful. But his editorial misgivings were strong: "Narcisse is one of your very best creations. The nurse—(of whom there is so little) is capital and the Dr. is a fine old fellow. Then the description of the beginning of the War is most valuable and excellent—but utterly thrown away in this 'tract.' "[11] In subsequent letters Gilder would repeat his encouragement for the "delicious" and the "artistic" in the minor characters (19 April 1882). But the politics distressed him. Cable, however, was just not ready to be steered in the direction of the romance of reconciliation. He was more concerned with the neglect of the freed Negro and his "case" than he was to perpetuate the "picturesque" depiction of the darky.[12] He had joined this struggle—to picture black character as a person rather than as some sort of charming inferior in *The Grandissimes*—several years earlier. He had withstood considerable editorial pressure then, and he stood firm again.

Into the 1880s, as the New South mentality grew into a vogue and the North tired of the problem of the freedman, Cable continued to worry the topic. *John March, Southerner* (1895), which might be considered his Reconstruction romance, alienated Gilder even more than *Dr. Sevier* had done:

> The mind is irritated continually and can never rest in any pleasantness—the spirit is not free to enjoy either the happiness or the *unhappiness* of the characters—everything seems to be *spoiled*—both the mirth and the misery seem to lack dignity and completeness. The best and most original character is the rascally semi-darkey; the reader does get some fun out of him.[13]

That everything seems spoiled because everything *is* spoiled did not occur to Gilder—as it failed to occur to Macmillan's George

Brett when he returned Grace King's *The Pleasant Ways of St. Médard*. *John March, Southerner* is indeed about the spoiling of the South in the aftermath of Reconstruction. Cornelius Leggett, "the rascally semi-darkey," is Cable's study of the freedman used by everyone for short-term financial and political advantage. Cable also shows that the southern land has become the prey of fast-talking swindlers who pose as the harbingers of industrial progress but bring only desolation and upheaval. Education is shown to be a political pork barrel and subterfuge. In the end everyone is disappointed. The old order of John March's eighteenth-century father has been turned out, and in the words of Parson Tombs, the elder March's contemporary, the new age is announced by " 'a red an' threatenin' dawn of another time, a time o'mines and mills an' fact'ries an' swarmin' artisans an' operatives an' all the concomitants o' crowded an' complicated conditions.' "[14] There is no Scarlett O'Hara figure to rise from the ashes of Twelve Oaks and prosper in the New South.

In *John March, Southerner*—a difficult book to read and by no means a successful novel—Cable dismantles the twin panaceas of the New South—Industry and Education. He shows that the healing of the rebellious South is largely a self-serving fiction of the carpetbaggers and others who would rather be relieved of the rigors of an authentic reconciliation. Throughout the novel, like the embodiment of Cable's own doubt and pessimism, broods the character of Jeff-Jack Ravenel, son of a landed squire, who never goes back to the old ways. Early in the novel he "fell to brooding on the impoverishment of eleven states, and on the hundreds of thousands of men and women sitting in the ashes of their desolated hopes and the lingering fear of unspeakable humiliations" [p. 16]. Like Rhett Butler, Jeff-Jack watches the "destruction of a civilization" and rides it out for his profit. The title character, John March, marries one of the few surviving belles and remains, like Ashley Wilkes, something of an ornament: striking to look at but more or less useless.

If Cable had been luckier with his novel of Reconstruction, perhaps he would have sold one million copies in six months. But his notion of the plight of the South was too demanding to fit a certain mold. An old order passes—and he shows that order as both foolish and honorable. A new order emerges—and his attitude toward it is also mixed. Jeff-Jack vies with John March for the central spot in the novel. But none of the intriguing flaws was counted as bad as Cable's failure to be "pleasant," to follow the recipe of North-South reconciliation with a happy romance. *John March, Southerner* did not sell.

Louis Rubin mourns Cable's defeat; Edmund Wilson seethes over his "strangulation."[15] A nearer contemporary, Edwin Mims, declared his early promise unfulfilled.[16] Cable did not regain the artistic elegance and power of his earlier writing. At least part of the reason is the deleterious effect of the recipe for southern literary reconstruction handed down from northern editors, critics, and publishers. This was an especially stringent part of the genteel code for literature, and it was reserved for southern writers. Hearn seems to have been almost immune. To him the skirmishing between southern writer and northern editor was a minor theater in a much more comprehensive war fought against the backdrop of large abstractions: ART and LUCRE. Particulars of region, recent history, politics—these dissolved in Hearn's exotic and wide-ranging imagination. He was much too fascinated with Finnish epics, Oriental folk tales, and Sanscrit legends to realize that there was an Old South, that some Yankees had trampled on it and were now, through a continuation of the war by other means, trying to prescribe a reconciliation flattering to themselves. Grace King is a truer indicator. Even though she cherished the Old South and her personal and cultural origin, she saw nothing wrong with the New as long as it confirmed her memories and assumptions about gentlemen, class, race, and good taste. Cable offers a much more interesting and complex picture. In the eyes of King and her friends, Cable sold out. But in Cable's work and correspondence we get a different view. He was a writer possessing a remarkable imagination and considerable skill. He was confronted with certain formulas and prototypes and was assured that these would bring him personal artistic success while fostering general social progress as well. But his imagination felt and his intellect knew differently. We know that the imagination was defeated, that the skill fell apart. But we also know—now—what he was up against.

Notes

1. Lafcadio Hearn, *Essays on American Literature*, ed. Sanki Ichikowa (Tokyo: Hokuseido Press, 1929), p. 67.

2. Lafcadio Hearn, "The Scenes of Cable's Romances," in George W. Cable, *Old Creole Days*, prologue by Edward Larocque Tinker (New York: Heritage Press, 1943), p. xix.

3. Letter to W. D. O'Connor, March 1884, in Elizabeth Bisland, *The Life and Letters of Lafcadio Hearn*, Vol. 1 (Boston: Houghton Mifflin, 1906), p. 319.

4. Grace King, *Memories of a Southern Woman of Letters* (New York: Macmillan, 1932), p. 58.

5. Letter to Charles Dudley Warner, 22 November 1885, in *Grace King of New Orleans: A Selection of Her Writings*, ed. Robert Bush (Baton Rouge: Louisiana State University Press, 1973), p. 379.

6. William Dean Howells, "Editor's Study," *Harper's Magazine*, June 1892, p. 156.

7. Grace King, *The Pleasant Ways of St. Médard* (New York: Henry Holt, 1916), p. 6.

8. Edward King, Letter to George W. Cable, 4 February 1874, Howard-Tilton Memorial Library, Tulane University.

9. Robert Underwood Johnson, Letter to George W. Cable, 2 December 1879, Howard-Tilton Memorial Library, Tulane University.

10. Robert Underwood Johnson, *Remembered Yesterdays* (Boston: Little, Brown, 1923), pp. 121–122.

11. Richard Watson Gilder, Letter to George W. Cable, 1 February 1882, Howard-Tilton Memorial Library, Tulane University.

12. George W. Cable, "The Freedman's Case in Equity," *Century*, January 1885, pp. 409–418.

13. Richard Watson Gilder, Letter to George W. Cable, 23 June 1893, Howard-Tilton Memorial Library, Tulane University.

14. George W. Cable, *John March, Southerner* (New York: Scribner's, 1895), p. 295.

15. Louis D. Rubin, Jr., *George W. Cable: The Life and Times of a Southern Heretic* (New York: Pegasus, 1969), p. 239; Edmund Wilson, *Patriotic Gore* (New York: Oxford University Press, 1962), p. 579.

16. Edwin Mims, *History of Southern Fiction* (Richmond: Southern Historical Publication Society, 1909), p. lxii.

Miriam J. Shillingsburg

The Ascent of Woman, Southern Style: Hentz, King, Chopin

When one considers the "role of woman" in nineteenth-century America, various stereotypes come to mind: the bustling New England matron, the political activist, and the plantation belle on a pedestal, to name only a few. Our common conception of the upper-class southern woman is that she was either satisfied with her position on the pedestal, or if not, as with Mary Boykin Chesnut, she dared not say so out loud. While both these conceptions are truthful ones, they do not tell the whole story of the southern woman, and particularly they do not accurately reveal her attitude toward her position. I find, rather, an undercurrent of discontent among nineteenth-century southern women, one that was voiced not only in private diaries, but at regular intervals in the extremely popular fiction that they wrote and read.

While many fewer women than men wrote, those who did write have been disproportionately neglected by scholars of southern literature. According to the most recent compilation of published scholarship on southern literature, only two women writers before 1865 were studied between 1968 and 1975.[1] These two attracted only biographical notices and publication of some primary material. In the postbellum period, only eight women attracted even one scholarly nod, with titles about Kate Chopin equalling the number attracted by all seven others combined, including Ellen Glasgow. The writings of these women are, at their worst, no worse than a host of writings by men who are studied. And at their best, these works can tell us much about the real feelings of half the population of the nineteenth century. Looking at three representative nineteenth-century women, we can discern a change in the women's own attitude toward themselves in the latter part of the century.

The three novels discussed in this paper show the ways in which three female characters bucked convention and their "place" in society, the reactions of those societies to their rebellion, and the degree of success each heroine (and quite likely each author) felt in being her own self in spite of the circumscriptions of being a female in the South. These widely read novels were written between 1852 and 1899 by women of differing social and marital experiences. Caroline Lee Hentz, author of *Eoline* (1852), died a married woman who had supported her children and ailing husband for several years by writing; spinster Grace Elizabeth King, her family impoverished by the Civil War, wrote her own fantasies of young women's restoration to their plantations followed by happy marriages; and Kate Chopin, whose 1899 *The Awakening* has lately received much attention from feminists, died a widow.

The novels of these women each have a female central character who, I believe, strongly reflects the authors' own experiences of rebellion and, to some extent perhaps, a sense of failure. It is significant, I think, that these authors use the arts—literature, music, and painting—as metaphors for meaningful achievement for southern women, for it is through art that a woman can capture and control her experiences. We see a definite movement from Hentz's antebellum romance in which the central character's defiance is merely a hook to hang a love plot on, to King's examination of the society's values during Reconstruction with love and marriage the proper reward for a young girl's acquiring the acceptable values, to Chopin's questioning the entire set of assumptions which underlay the relationships between men and women. But if these women used their fiction for self-examination, as I suspect they did, their society seems never to have examined itself.

Eoline; or, Magnolia Vale[2] gives a typical representation of Mrs. Hentz's female character. In spite of its conventional plotting and characterization, it contains nevertheless an obvious undercurrent of discontent and latent feminism. Planter Kingsly Glenmore has contrived with his neighbor that his daughter Eoline should marry

Mr. Cleveland's son Horace. Even though Horace "has consented to obey his father" and marry Eoline, she "can imagine nothing so dreadful as the loveless union" she believes her father intends to force on her [p. 21]. The issue then becomes solely one of "filial disobedience" opposed to paternal "authority." Mrs. Hentz makes clear this conflict both dramatically and through authorial commentary. When the father insists, for example, " 'I do love you—I do wish your happiness; and I know better than yourself, how to secure it. You will thank me, one day, for the authority I now exert. Eoline, you must obey me in this. You must marry Horace Cleveland' " [p. 10], the author says that Mr. Glenmore

> knew of no sovereign more absolute than his own will. . . . That Eoline, so gentle, and yielding in all minor things, so childlike and affectionate in her daily demeanor, so attentive to all the sweet courtesies of life, so anxious to please him in the minutest particular . . . should now undauntedly brave his authority, resist his will, and thwart the favorite plan he had been maturing from her infancy—he could not, would not believe. [pp. 10–11]

The conflict of wills reaches its climax in the first chapter when the father gives Eoline an ultimatum:

> ". . . if you persist in this rebellion, I will no longer consider you as my daughter. . . . The independence in which you glory, shall be your only inheritance. I will neither share my home, nor my fortune, with an ingrate who mocks at my authority, and resists my will. This is the alternative—choose this moment. On one side, wealth, talents, influence, friends, and favor—on the other, poverty, disgrace, and banishment." [p. 11]

When the daughter chooses "poverty and banishment—it cannot be disgrace," her father calls her "insufferable," "insolent," and "enough to drive one mad" [p. 11].

Several points applicable to the other books I shall discuss should be made about Eoline's conflict. First, Eoline is an heiress, an upper-class woman, and therefore she *does* have a choice. Lower-class southern females, in these books and others, and, apparently, in real life, had no choice. It is important, however, for Eoline and her spiritual sisters who would oppose the system that the only choice was to fall down the social ladder and in the process, of course, off the pedestal. This is made explicit first by the compliments of a European traveller who "wished [she] were the daughter of a poor man, so that [she] might be compelled to give [her] voice to the world" [p. 6], and then by her father's ruminations about Eoline's new position in a female seminary: ". . . shall she be made a musical drudge, a hireling, a slave. . . . who plunges herself into banishment and degradation" [p. 23]. When her employer incorrectly assumes that she has "been taught by eminent masters . . . educated for a music teacher," Eoline agrees that it was "family misfortunes, I presume?" which forced her to become a teacher [pp. 53–54]. Still Eoline, unlike the women who live in vulgar cabins, does not have to work; she can instead marry Horace Cleveland and double her fortune, if not her pleasure. Instead, however, the defiant Eoline goes from a bad situation into a worse one.

Secondly, Eoline's conflict is the traditional one of the powerful versus the powerless, in this case specifically represented in the twofold symbol of male-female and father-child. Eoline must walk a figurative tightrope between achieving too much power, becoming unfeminine, and remaining too passive, languishing into apathy. She is, therefore, juxtaposed to two models of female behavior, the first of whom, Miss Manly, is the strong-willed owner of the seminary; the second, the passive, ghost-like Amelia. Although nothing of Miss Manly's past is known, she appears to be a self-made woman (like Mrs. Hentz). Eoline had "hoped to have found in Miss Manly the guardianship of a mother, and the tenderness of a friend" [p. 44], but instead she found "a wonderful disciplinarian, and as she conduct[ed] her school with true military order, and as she [had] . . . a commanding appearance, [the students] call[ed] her the Colonel" [p. 70]. Later, however, we discover that "Miss Manly was not that *strange anomaly*, a woman without a heart, which Eoline had at first supposed her to be. She had a heart, though covered with a coat of mail" [p. 98].

It is clear that Col. Manly's problem is not her strong will but the lack of "all softer emotions" [p. 188]. When the young romantic St. Leon languishes, "trembling on the verge of death" [p. 183] from "an affection of the heart" [p. 189], Eoline's promise to marry him saves his life. The specific comparison between the heroine and Col. Manly (who is enamoured of St. Leon) is made by one of the children: "Miss Manly is kind and devoted, but she lacks the softness and gentleness of womanhood, *she* is wanting in what Nature has lavished on *you*" [p. 202]. Although Hentz's point is that a woman's will must be tempered by tenderness, she also warns her readers about the dangers of passivity.

The daughter of Glenmore's friend, Amelia (née) Wilton provides the second negative role model. Though formerly as beautiful as Eoline, she has become a walking ghost, the result of "a loveless, ill-assorted marriage . . . that has frozen the fountains of youthful feelings, paralized [*sic*] the spring of youthful energy, and turned her heart to stone" [p. 113]. Wilton explains to Glenmore that Amelia

> "had but one fault—a too yielding temper. Ever swayed by the will of others, ever sacrificing her own wishes to those around her, it was impossible to discover whether she had a wish or will of her own. . . . We encouraged her to lean on her own judgment, to think, feel and act for herself, but she never would do it." [pp. 113–114]

At last, when sought in marriage, Amelia's response was " 'I am willing to marry him if you think it best that I should' " [p. 114].

Hentz makes the theme of the powerful versus the powerless clear throughout this her first novel, but in 1852 she must have felt the necessity for a conventional ending. That is, Eoline and Horace *do* marry, apparently to live happily ever after. But it is only after defiance of her parent, loss of her cherished privacy, a narrow escape from her pledge to marry the dying young man, and numerous other complications of honor, duty, will, pride, and love, that she discovers the merits of her neighbor, thereby fulfilling her father's will.

Thirdly, the way a southern lady expressed her *self* seems to have been not through her choice of mate, nor pride in her children, certainly not in a "career" however loosely defined, not even through pride in domestic work. Rather the respectable outlet open to such a woman seems to have been only through the arts. Eoline excels in singing and playing stringed instruments, and while at her father's home she has no other apparent interests but reading. When turned out of Eden, Eoline becomes a music teacher, often finding an outlet for sadness or pleasure in her music. In short, as Hentz develops this theme, music is an expression of Eoline's self, not a way of making a living, although fortunately the two functions do overlap for our heroine.

The author herself saw as the major theme of the book Eoline's resisting "the immolation of her principles and her feelings"; and it is that, Hentz states, which "exalts [her] into a heroine, and as such her history is worthy to be recorded" [p. 16]. She reiterates this theme of individual principle in many voices; for example, Eoline tells Wilton "When a young lady is forced to act independently . . . she is very apt to incur the censure of the world. Strength of principle may be mistaken for obstinancy, and self-reliance be branded as self-will" [p. 206]. Likewise St. Leon is unacceptable to Eoline because he lacks a "manly spirit" (that is, he is not as strong-willed as Eoline); therefore, she makes a match between him and the passive Amelia. And finally Horace Cleveland says that they love each other "as we always would have done had we been left to our own free will" [p. 250].

Thus the story of a rather unconventional young woman has a conventional ending. In Mrs. Hentz's enormously popular works, such a girl is usually the central figure, and in her later novels this heroine pushes farther and farther the limits of convention. Hentz's latest volumes carried such bittersweet titles as *Courtship and Marriage; or Joys and Sorrows of American Life* and *Love After Marriage*, and the way she could get by with writing this kind of latent feminism is that she gives her upper-class heroines a happy ending. As long as Love Conquers All and All's Well That Ends Well, people were not "turned off" by a strident feminist message. Her tactic seems to have been to push out and then retreat. Whereas a woman like Margaret Fuller in Boston received damning reviews for her straightforward protest, *Woman in the Nineteenth Century,* Mrs. Hentz's books were bought and read, perhaps merely reinforcing the *status quo*, perhaps subtly inciting young girls to rebellion to try to free themselves from cultural enslavement to male authority.

Unlike Mrs. Hentz, who was mainly writing conventional romantic plots of aristocratic boy-marries-aristocratic girl, Grace Elizabeth King is more interested in the psychological motivation of her characters. In the topsy-turvy world of postbellum New Orleans, she became one of the earliest writers in America to chronicle a young woman's initiation into the adult world. She is primarily interested in the acquisition of the values—racial, social, and marital—of the late adolescent female, the young woman reaching the age when she would have to make the crucial decision on marriage. King is concerned not only with *what* those values are, but also with *how* they are acquired Her first book, *Monsieur Motte* (1888), a series of four related stories which treats seriously the initiation of Marie Modeste into womanhood, shows a character imbedded in a specific time and place, and largely controlled by that time and place.[3] In this sense, King is moving from the romanticism of Hentz to the psychological realism of Kate Chopin and other writers a decade later.

In the first story "Monsieur Motte,"the black hairdresser Marcélite gathers for the orphaned Marie Modeste's graduation ball the required silk dancing boots, white gown, and the gloves, on behalf of Marie's uncle Monsieur Motte, who it is believed has supported the niece during her ten years at boarding school. He is to arrive from his business on the afternoon of the ball which eventually will lead to her marriage. However, when the ceremony is over and Marie Modeste has not yet seen this uncle, she recognizes her plight as a woman without a protector:

> What had her weak little body not endured in patient ignorance? But the others were not ignorant,—the teachers, Marcélite, her uncle! . . . She saw it now, and she felt a woman's indignation and pity over it. . . . She leaned her head against the side of her bed and wept, not for herself, but for all women and all orphans. [p. 78–79]

The next morning when the headmistress and Marie vainly seek an explanation for the uncle's absence, Marcélite is nowhere to be found. Days later a drunken and disheveled Marcélite staggers back to the school, confessing "But don't tell my *bébé*, don't let her know. My God! It will kill her! She's got no uncle—no Monsieur Motte! It was all a lie. It was me,—me a nigger, that sent her to school and paid for her—"[p. 96].

The real issue becomes clear when Marie asks to be taken home with Marcélite, although the headmistress has promised her a place teaching at the school. Marcélite recognizes the problem instantly—it having been her own concern all these years: "Go to my home! A white young lady like you go live with a nigger like me! . . . What!

You don't think you ain't white! Oh, God! Strike me dead!"[pp. 100-101].

Fortunately the black hairdresser can produce the proper documentation, "a little worn-out prayer-book, but all filled with written papers and locks of hair and dates and certificates,—frail fluttering scraps that dropped all over the table, but unanswerable champions for the honor of dead men and the purity of dead women"[p. 102]. The two final paragraphs of the story show black and white women clasping hands and the resolution is perfect—because Marie is, after all, pure white.

In 1885 King wrote in a letter to her sister:

> It seems to me, white as well as black women have a sad showing in what some people call romance. I am very tired, and I should think others are too, of these local stories, but as I recollect little things, I think I shall try and write them. If no one else does it better, one of these days they may prove a pleasant record and serve to bring us all nearer together blacks and whites.[4]

The important things about this story are, I think, exactly what King said they were—bringing the women of two races together and displaying the love and depth of emotion they share in defiance of their culture. Of course, it is the black woman who defies the culture by supporting the white child—giving her a chance in the finest boarding school available. The white woman, as the culture demands, must remain ignorant of her benefactress. Still Marie shows considerable respect and affection for Marcélite without having an overt reason to do so. But a hundred years later we find the ending a cop-out, a backing off from facing the real issue: the white Marie's ambiguous relationship with the black Marcélite. But the requirements of the society and of the reading public were that she be found pure white; and apparently King herself condoned that position.

But what is more important is that the author is exploring the values—and some of them are racial—of a seventeen-year-old girl. What would have happened if Marcélite had been unable to produce the worn prayerbook? If she had been required to "go home with" the Negress, what would her life have been like? To what extent is the shaping influence in the young girl's life the attempt to please the fictitious uncle? Or worst of all, what if Marcélite had merely reared the white child herself as perhaps the dying mother had actually expected her to do? These questions are not answered by King, but at least in an oblique fashion she has asked them. She has made a tentative step toward remedying the "sad showing in what some people call romance" of both black and white women, especially of the adolescent.

In the second chapter of *Monsieur Motte*, King rather explicitly ascribes Marie's problems to the fact that she is a woman. While Hentz's heroine is the inferior mainly because of a parent-child relationship rather than a male-female one, King makes it very clear that women have some problems *because* they are women: their mercurial dispositions and the inability of women whether black or white to control their own lives are named particularly. When Marie spends the summer on a sugar plantation, the mistress, impressed with Marie's naive joy, comments:

> Why must women be always looking for the unattainable,—why cannot we be contented? . . . if it is the will of God, why must we have these feelings, these moments . . . ? She will crave to know it, and then, like me, she will crave acquittance of the knowledge and the refreshment of ignorance again. It is always with us women the fight between the heart and the soul. [p. 143]

Marie believes she has "no future" because she has "no home, no husband, no children . . . no pleasure." At times she felt "martyrdom the only proper vocation of women" [p. 148], for "She was at the pitiable age [King tells us] when sensitiveness is a disease, before moral courage has had time to develop" [p. 149]. While the adolescent Marie broods, she gives the "silent treatment" to her *bonne* Marcélite, who longs for "one moment of equality and confidence!" [p. 150]. The destinies of women in the Creole society, Grace King says, are "suprise-boxes to us women; we never know what is going to come out of them: our own plans, our own ideas count for nothing. . . . Men are the serious occupation, women are the playthings, of fate" [pp. 158–159].

In the book's third segment, Marie Modeste meets her future husband, Charles Montyon who, in the fourth story, discovers that he is not the rightful owner of his plantation, nor the legal one; however, after suitable complications, Marie discovers that the plantation in question rightfully and legally belongs to her. Therefore, at age eighteen, orphan Marie Modeste Motte has "bought into" the culture. She has confirmed her pure white heritage, acquired the undying affection of her faithful Negro nurse, recovered her lost plantation complete with family portraits and plate, and found the man who earlier was willing to love her even without dowery; and in the postbellum society she is ready to marry him—a businessman, not a planter—solely for love. Once again, the story has a happy ending; yet in this book Grace King examines the treatment of women by their society in a more specific and personal way than did Hentz in *Eoline*, where nothing is assumed wrong about the society itself or its values. Although King's attitude on race was patronizing, if not actually racist as we would understand the term, she nevertheless showed genuine affection between the fictional women of the two races. And if she did show the young white woman finally accepting the values of her society, it is not without self-searching and growth.[5] A decade later Marie might have found a sister in Edna Pontellier, who had also married a New Orleans businessman when she was about twenty, but for whom the romantic dream was to become merely an illusion.

Feminists and others have recently discovered Edna in Kate Chopin's astounding novel, *The Awakening*, published in 1899.[6] It is the story, on the obvious level, of a young wife's awakening to sexual love outside her marriage. But at deeper levels it is the awakening of the self of Edna Pontellier in conflict with the culture, symbolized in part by Edna's stirring appreciation of music and by her fledgling attempts to paint.

Chopin's biographers agree that she had had a happy marriage with six children when her husband died in Kate's thirty-second year, in 1883. About five years later she began to write "hesitatingly," and her earliest work is known mainly for its local color characteristics.[7] Many of her works center on a strong, determined young woman, often a wife, who rebels against husband and society; but the endings of these stories are varied so as not to put forward a single solution for the "place" of women. One of the protagonists runs away from home only to return at the discovery of her impending motherhood; another only wants to spend some money frivolously; one converts from tomboy to feminine mystique.

However, with Edna, Chopin wrote what seems today a thoroughly honest account of a woman at odds with her society's values. This central figure is, like Eoline and Marie, an upper-class woman, the wife of a highly respected Creole businessman Léonce Pontellier. Because she is by upbringing a Presbyterian, Edna is unused to the customs of the less introspective, more free-wheeling Creole wives who spend their summers on Grand Isle. When Robert Lebrun flirts with them, they warn him that Edna "might make the unfortunate blunder of taking [him] seriously" [2:900]. And soon Robert and Edna appear to be in love. Therefore, Edna must make some choices; but once again they are not entirely free ones, and Edna suffers in consequence. She chooses "the inward life which questions" rather than "the outward existence which conforms" to society's requirements [2:893].

Edna's struggle is symbolized most specifically by her relationship with her husband and with her father. The night after she first heard Mademoiselle Reisz play Chopin, followed by her learning to swim "where no woman had swum before" [2:908], Edna falls asleep in the hammock. When Léonce asks her to come to bed, she declines, although "another time she would have . . . yielded to his desire . . . unthinkingly" [2:912]. But now, "she perceived that her will blazed up, stubborn and resistant. She could not at that moment have done other than denied and resisted" [2:912].

Later, Edna breaks the ritual which she "had religiously followed since her marriage, six years before," by not receiving her Tuesday callers [2:932]. When Léonce asks her reason, she replies, "I simply felt like going out, and I went out. . . . I left no excuse. I told Joe to say I was out, and that was all" [2:932]. Léonce's only concern—like the later one when she moves out of his house—is that snubbing wives and daughters will adversely affect his business deals. She can resist, but finally she is powerless. The chapter concludes as Edna flings her wedding ring, the symbol of her bondage, "upon the carpet . . . stamped her heel upon it, striving to crush it. But her small boot heel did not make an indenture" [2:934]. Her lack of power is obvious when, at her maid's bidding, she replaces the ring on her finger. Likewise, Edna's relationship with her father has placed her in a powerless position, although by the time he visits her in New Orleans she has largely escaped his influence. He was "convinced . . . that he had bequeathed to all his daughters the germs of a masterful capability, which only depended upon their own efforts to be directed toward successful achievement" [2:950]; and, although she had defied him when she married Léonce six years ago, his influence on her personality had been considerable.

However, through art, Edna is able to control her father both literally and symbolically. As she sketches his portrait, "he sat rigid and unflinching, as he had faced the cannon's mouth in days gone by . . . he motioned [the children] away with an expressive action of the foot, loath to disturb the fixed lines of his countenance, his arms, or his rigid shoulders" [2:950–951]. Literally, then, she makes him rigid, unmovable, confined; and symbolically she shapes him by the act of painting his portrait. In a rather complex symbol, Chopin allows Edna to capture and control her world in painting just as Mlle. Reisz captivates the sensitive with her music. In fact, the courage of the artist is consistently stressed in the image of the bird which soars "above the level plain of tradition and prejudice" [2:966]. Art, then, is an acceptable way—because it appears harmless—for women to express their *selves* in this society, but, as Mlle. Reisz knows well, to succeed as an artist, one "must possess the courageous soul. . . . The soul that dares and defies" [2:946]. Therefore, fortuitously, Edna's artistic temperament and her restless spirit symbolically complement each other. Edna awakens to her true self and defies her society.

However, in 1899 the nation was not ready for an "awakened" woman, and Chopin knew this. Although younger and more charming than Edna's husband, Robert her lover is not ready to meet her needs. He admits that he tried not to love her because, he says, "you were not free; you were Léonce Pontellier's wife. . . . I was demented, dreaming of wild, impossible things, recalling men who had set their wives free" [2:991-992]. Edna's reply:

> "You have been a very, very foolish boy, wasting your time dreaming of impossible things when you speak of Mr. Pontellier setting me free! I am no longer one of Mr. Pontellier's possessions to dispose of or not. I give myself where I choose. If he were to say, 'Here, Robert, take her and be happy; she is yours,' I should laugh at you both." [2:992]

While Edna attends a birth—another complicated metaphor—Robert leaves a note: "I love you. Good-by—because I love you"

[2:997]. Unable either to think of "having" Edna without possessing her, or perhaps to face the censure of society in a divorce or an open love affair, Robert deserts the woman he loves telling himself it is *because* he loves her. Consequently, in an act of obvious defiance, Edna disrobes and walks into the sea while a bird with a broken wing reels and flutters down to the water. Edna's final vision as she drowns is of her father, who in his military uniform is a symbol of authority, discipline, and restraint.

Chopin's literary career ended with Edna's suicide. Readers and critics were not yet ready for her honesty and courage in expressing the needs of a woman who refused to obey the restrictive social conventions of the times. Juxtaposed against the fictional lives of an Eoline or a Marie Modeste (and most other protagonists of Hentz or King), Edna Pontellier's emotional honesty—her refusing to submit to the male-defined stereotype—achieves sharp focus. The juxtaposition, of course, provides sufficient reason for our taking a serious critical look at the work of Hentz, King, and other minor women writers of the nineteenth century; for it is through their vision that we can understand and define the dynamics of the reaction against stereotype in life as well as in fiction of the nineteenth century.

However, in the twentieth century, women in southern fiction begin to see that they have alternatives. They can remain unmarried for one thing, as is brilliantly demonstrated in Frances Newman's *The Hard-Boiled Virgin* (1926). But without the early stories of the Hentzes and Kings, perhaps there would not yet have been a Chopin, a Newman, certainly not a Flannery O'Connor, whose stories simply do not have to deal with the relationships between men and women as cultural phenomena. O'Connor's barnyard seductions are not sexual acts but spiritual ones; the characters are not merely men and women but forces of evil and good in the world. Only when a culture can "get over" or beyond a primary interest in sexual mores, can acts between the sexes become symbolic actions. These neglected southern women writers provide a context and a heritage in which to view the achievement and promise of their successors.

Notes

1. Jerry T. Williams, ed., *Southern Literature 1968–1975: A Checklist of Scholarship* (Boston: G. K. Hall, 1978).

2. Caroline Lee Hentz, *Eoline; or, Magnolia Vale* (Philadelphia: T. B. Peterson, 1852; rpt, Freeport, N.Y.: Books for Libraries Series, 1971).

3. Grace Elizabeth King, *Monsieur Motte* (Freeport, N.Y.: Books for Libraries Series, 1969).

4. Robert Bush, ed., *Grace King of New Orleans* (Baton Rouge: Louisiana State University Press, 1973), p. 14.

5. See Marie Fletcher, "Grace Elizabeth King: Her Delineation of the Southern Heroine," *Louisiana Studies* 5 (Spring 1966): 50–60.

6. Kate Chopin, *The Awakening*, ed. Per Seyersted, *The Complete Works of Kate Chopin,* Vol. 2 (Baton Rouge: Louisiana State University Press, 1969), pp. 879–1000.

7. Seyersted, "Introduction," 1:22.

Thomas Bonner, Jr.

Kate Chopin: Tradition and the Moment

When Kate Chopin began to write in the 1880s, many authors in the South, not the least of whom were women, were involved in making apologies for the Lost Cause. Grace King and Ruth McEnery Stuart were notable guardians of the French civilizations—Creole and Acadian—in Louisiana. However, Kate Chopin, like George Washington Cable, perceived that a decisive change already had occurred and that more changes were to come. Addressing herself to the social milieu of post–Civil War French Louisiana, Chopin suggested that the bonds of caste had been broken and that a freer society was in the process of formation. Her literary efforts move from a broad analysis of society to a study of relations between the sexes and finally focus on the individual and the demands of selfhood.

As Emerson, Thoreau, and Margaret Fuller had two generations earlier in New England, Chopin raised troublesome issues of self and society. These proved too difficult for genteel readers and critics of the Gilded Age, eventually resulting in her literary estrangement followed by an untimely death and critical obscurity. Over a half century elapsed before Kenneth Eberle in 1964 brought out a reprint of *The Awakening*. But by 1969, when Per Seyersted published her complete works, a new-found audience welcomed her message. Readers of the 1960s and 1970s found that Chopin had created "modern" characters who frequently break the bonds of tradition for the demands of the moment. Her exploration of themes of caste, race, sex, and self reveals her as a writer who, though reared in a convent school, speaks not for the past but to the present.

In Chopin's first major publication, *At Fault* (1890), the emphasis is on change as a condition of reality. The recently widowed Thérèse Lafirme is faced with conflicts ranging from the regional to the domestic to the personal as she learns to run the plantation on her own. She must confront the presence of northern industrial interests that have invaded the pastoral sanctuary of Place du Bois with a railroad and lumber mill. Also, she must face up to her feelings for Hosmer, the manager of the mill, as she grows to love him, and accept his being divorced as an impediment to their marriage. Thérèse is an instance of the decisive female character that Chopin is to experiment with in her early fiction and develop fully in *The Awakening*. She proves able to enter the man's world of running the plantation and to accept the changes to the land and culture that come with "industrial progress." Her ability to accommodate change stands in stark contrast to that of her nephews Grégoire and Joçint, whose only response is violence ending in death. Also, in the tide of emotion sweeping through her romance with Hosmer, she does not allow her system of values to be undermined. She adheres to the Roman Catholic teaching on divorce but also touches on an idea that becomes a major focus in *The Awakening*, asserting that moral principle finally is "something peculiarly one's own."[1]

While *At Fault* realistically depicts the flux of French society in and about Natchitoches, Louisiana, *Bayou Folk* explores change in a far more comprehensive manner. This remarkable collection of stories, published in 1894, examines in a thoroughgoing way the mix of Creoles, Acadians, mulattoes, Negroes, poor whites, and Texans who live in a small area of the South. Here a sophisticated caste system operates, the effects of which are to prevent change and preserve traditional patterns of living. "In and Out of Old Natchitoches" ambitiously seeks to probe through these evolving complexities of race and society. Alphonse Laballière, who has left his brother's sugar plantation along the lower Mississippi River to come up to Natchitoches, restore a plantation, and plant cotton, attains a growing racial tolerance. When he moves to the plantation, he decides not to dislodge a family of mulattoes living in the ruin of the main house. Rather, he dines with them and stays in a small outbuilding. But he remains concerned with society's demand for moral appearances and resents criticism of his actions. Angered by local complaints about his close relationship with the mulattoes, he impulsively tries to enroll a young black boy in a white school on his property. The child is promptly denied admission.

Despite her bold handling of racial themes, however, Chopin's treatment remains somewhat ambiguous. The narrator describes Alphonse's bringing the youth to the school as "stupid." It is not clear whether she finds Alphonse's actions hotheaded and cruel to the child who is put in this humiliating situation, or whether she thinks integration is itself a blunder or at least premature. Chopin, like her characters, seems caught in the shifting tides of racial change and not entirely certain of her course. But unlike other authors of the period, she does not shy away from dealing openly with this volatile issue.

In *A Night in Acadie* (1897), Chopin moves in another controversial direction—toward the theme of erotic awakening. Robert Bender observes, "Variations on the themes of awakening to ecstatic self-realization, her stories are fictional songs of the self. In them, she affirms apsects of the self that conventions denied, affirms them in a way that resembles Whitman when he sings approvingly of 'forbidden voices, / Voices of sexes and lusts.' "[2] Chopin's focus on eroticism is important not only in substance but also in manner. Her open treatment, often compared with Flaubert's, suggests that eroticism is intrinsic to human nature and has an important bearing on human feelings, ideas, and actions. But, in *Madame Bovary*, Flaubert makes the reader feel that there is something wrong with Emma's sexual desires. One does not perceive that impression in Chopin's handling of the subject; her work implies an often empathetic attitude.

"A Sentimental Soul" and "At Chênière Caminada" explore the passion of one person for another, with the complication that the desired relationship is prohibited by custom. Fleurette in "A Sentimental Soul" falls in love with Lacodie, a married man. Stifling a storm of emotion, she is wracked with guilt and tortured in her attempts to expiate it. Chopin points out how normal the attraction between a man and a woman is and yet how abnormal are rituals and customs which repress the emotions, as in this story when

Fleurette is able to love Lacodie only after he is dead and his widow remarried.

Unlike this story, in which religious customs form the repressing force, "At Chênière Caminada" finds Tonie, a young Acadian, in love with an upper-class Creole girl whose social status precludes his making any serious declaration of his love. Claire's playing an old church organ which had been silent for years foreshadows Tonie's romantic inclinations, which also appear in Chopin's use of imagery (a major consideration in *The Awakening*): "Some days he wanted to see how she spread her bare, white arms, and walked to meet the foam-crested waves" [1:313]. Tonie's taking Claire on his boat for a solitary voyage becomes simultaneously the attainment of his goal and the unfortunate moment of truth, when his desire is defeated by Claire's offering him a tip: "I have no money tonight, Tonie; take this [silver chain] instead" [1:315].

In "Athénaïse" and "A Respectable Woman," Chopin continues her exploration of the erotic theme with an increase in sexual realism. Athénaïse, a young bride of an older husband, a widower of ten years, fails to have her romantic expectations fulfilled. She bolts from his home after two months, staying first at her parents' home and later at a guest house in New Orleans. There she meets the suave Gouvernail, who fires her passion, so much so that when she discovers that she is pregnant by her husband, she feels a warmth and attraction for her spouse that she had never before experienced. Psychologically and emotionally, Gouvernail achieves for her what her husband had not been able to and she returns to her husband as the complete lover: "Her whole passionate nature was aroused as if by a miracle" [1:451]. Chopin also describes the gentleman's arousal and his wishes to "soothe her, do her bidding, whatever it might be" [1:447].

"A Respectable Woman" is an ironic exploration of the awakening of sexual passion in Mrs. Baroda, who at first rejects Gouvernail without having met him. Her initial response to news of his visit reveals that her fears are less from without than within, for she is not unlike Hawthorne's Faith in "Young Goodman Brown" when she asks her husband not to leave her alone this one night of the year. To avoid temptation, she plans to go to New Orleans, but the evening before her departure she meets Gouvernail in the garden.

"The approaching red point of a lighted cigar" [1:335] signals both his approach and the moment of temptation. Bringing her a filmy white scarf for the cool evening and romantically murmuring a few lines from Whitman, he begins an intimate, philosophical conversation about his present and past and disarms her defensive reflexes: "She wanted to draw close to him and whisper against his cheek—she did not care what—as she might have done if she had not been a respectable woman" [1:335].

This awakening has more to do with sexuality than with love and prefigures the sexual arousal without accompaniment of love in *The Awakening*. The dark-and-light imagery throughout "A Respectable Woman" intimates the moral forces at play; but the red tip of the cigar, like Faith's pink ribbons, suggests the great power of the flesh and the complexity surrounding the conflict. The most startling moment of the narrative occurs in the delightfully ambiguous conclusion after Mrs. Baroda's return from the city; she speaks to her husband of Gouvernail: "I have overcome everything! You will see. This time I will be very nice to him" [1:336]. The ambivalence of the ending is significant because the stories exploring the theme of awakened sensibilities suggest questions rather than answers, beginnings rather than endings.

Although Chopin had planned a third collection of stories, *A Vocation and a Voice*, she was never able to find a publisher. Fifty-one stories remained uncollected at the time of her death, and many were unpublished. The limitations of popular taste and the bold themes of the stories often prevented editors and publishers from accepting them. For example, "Ti Dimon," which reflects passions in violation of morality, was rejected by the *Atlantic*.[3] Although these stories share some of the interests and forms of those in her two collections, they tend to develop characters who are strong individuals and to examine their lives as they conflict with the institutions around them.

Chopin in her earlier fiction had shown an awareness of the symbolic character, particularly in the stories which suggest an initiation theme. In these posthumously collected stories, a character is often poised for a moment in transition between two states of life, not necessarily chronological. The character, usually female, reaches a crisis, at which point she must exercise her will to assume her next role. Unlike Blake's Thel, who retreats from experience, Chopin's women, after deliberation or struggle, plunge into more active states of being.

In "Wiser than a God," Paula Von Stoltz chooses to pursue a profession as a musician rather than accept the orthodox role of wife. Marianne of "The Maid of Saint Phillipe," after the death of her father and the arrival of the news that the British are coming, chooses to venture into the wilderness to make a life of her own. In "A Pair of Silk Stockings," Mrs. Summers decides to spend money on her desires rather than on "necessities." The woman caught between the needs of motherhood and self becomes a symbolic concern in *The Awakening*.

Themes of self-determination and personal liberty emerge clearly in this large body of stories. Chopin often describes a rugged individuality reminiscent of Emerson, with whose works she was acquainted—in *The Awakening*, she portrays Edna Pontellier reading Emerson (and falling asleep). In his critical biography, Seyersted emphasizes the theme of woman's self-assertion and calls attention to the appearance of emancipated women. While a number of Chopin's stories stress the theme of female self-assertion, her fiction works toward a deeper, even cosmic concern for the self. In "Self-Reliance," Emerson writes, "I must be myself. I cannot break myself any longer for you. If you can love me for what I am, we shall be the happier. If you cannot, I will still seek to deserve that you should. I will not hide my tastes or aversions."[4] And it is this view which Chopin's female protagonists often explore—not only as women but also as representative human beings.

These characters place the demands of self before those of society. In one of her earliest literary efforts, "Emancipation: A Life Fable," a beast born in a cage escapes. Regardless of its problems in fending for itself, it finds compensation in the newly discovered liberty: "So does he live, seeking, finding, joying, and suffering. The door which accident had opened is open still, but the cage remains forever empty" [1:38]. In "Wiser than a God," when Paula is asked why she cannot marry, she replies, "Because it doesn't enter into the purpose of my life." Her inner drive and self-knowledge conquer not only the affection which she feels for her suitor but also the pressures of society in its advocacy of marriage. Chopin emphasizes Paula's wisdom with an epigraph prefixed to the story: "To love and be wise is scarcely granted even to a god" [1:39].

In "A Point at Issue," Charles Faraday, a professor of mathematics, and Eleanor Gail, a young woman with "broad views of life and humanity" [1:49] decide to marry, but they see their marriage as an opportunity to enlarge their individual lives free from the confining values ordinarily associated with the institution: "Each was to remain a free integral of humanity, responsible to no dominating exactions of so-called marriage laws" [1:50]. Shortly after the wedding, Charles arranges for Eleanor to reside alone in Paris in order to attain the cultural advantages which she missed in childhood: "Marriage, which marks too often the closing period of a woman's intellectual existence, was to be in her case the open portal through which she might seek the embellishments that her strong, graceful mentality deserved" [1:50]. Despite some difficulties, the marriage prevails in the original spirit.

Chopin explores a deeply repressed desire for personal liberty in "The Story of an Hour," in which a husband who was thought to be dead turns up alive. At first upset at the news that her husband has been killed in a train wreck, the wife retreats to her room to cope with her grief. Suddenly, she begins to experience a change: "She said it over and over under her breath: 'free, free, free'" [1:353]. Certainly an unorthodox response to a husband's "death," the reaction suggests the perseverance of a spirit despite the bonds of matrimony. As an institution which can restrict liberty, marriage is representative of the general institutions confining society, and the protagonist is a creature in revolt: "There would be no powerful will bending hers in that blind persistence with which men and women believe they have a right to impose a private will upon a fellow creature" [1:353]. However, when word is brought that her husband is alive, she dies of shock.

The Awakening, published in 1899, continues these thematic concerns for self-determination and personal liberty as well as the often-discussed theme of sexual awakening.[5] In her creation of Léonce Pontellier, however, Chopin offers an additional dimension—she examines the imposition of one's will upon another. She also depicts the institution of business as an impediment to personal growth. Chopin attacks not only the customs of Creole businessmen but also the absentee role of husbands in family life. She never fails to indicate the power and influence possessed by Léonce in his family as well as his business.

Léonce is a conventional, successful businessman, with competitive economic and social instincts which take precedence over his sensibilities. Unable or unwilling (one is never quite sure) to give of himself to his wife and sons, he compensates with expensive and timely gifts as means of continuing his influence during his absences. Such tactics meet with public approval: "And the ladies, selecting with dainty and discriminating fingers and a little greedily, all declared that Mr. Pontellier was the best husband in the world. Mrs. Pontellier was forced to admit that she knew of none better" [2:887]. The ladies' response is quite natural, even the hyperbole, but the key word *forced* suggests that Léonce's gifts are exertions less of beneficence than of power.

Léonce manages his household as an employer and assumes that all within will conduct themselves accordingly. He reproaches Edna for neglecting the children when one becomes ill: "If it was not a mother's place to look after the children, whose on earth was it: He himself had his hands full with the brokerage business" [2:885]. His home reflects his business prowess, a reason why he is so insistent about Edna's maintaining the Tuesday ritual of receiving callers. One thinks of Browning's Duke when Chopin writes:

> Mr. Pontellier was very fond of walking about his house examining its various appointments and details, to see that nothing was amiss. He greatly valued his possessions, chiefly because they were his, and derived genuine pleasure from contemplating a painting, a statuette, a rare lace curtain—no matter what—after he had brought it out and placed it among his household gods. [2:931]

He includes his wife among these "gods." He responds with disapproval when he notices that his wife has failed to wear the elaborate gown which the Tuesday visits demanded. Earlier, when Edna comes from the beach sunburned, he is irritated by her appearance: " 'You are burnt beyond recognition,' he added, looking at his wife as one looks at a valuable piece of personal property which has suffered some damage" [2:882]. When Edna moves from the family home to the pigeon house, he publicizes the arrival of architects and tradesmen who will refurbish the home while the family prepares to go abroad: "Mr. Pontellier had saved appearances" [2:977]. Characteristically, his last presence in the novel is by letter. With the characterization of Léonce, Chopin looks toward the Babbit of the 1920s and the contemporary "man in the grey flannel suit."

In *The Man of Letters in New England and the South*, Lewis P. Simpson writes of the post–Civil War South: "Now at last the writer is himself to become a redemptive figure in the fulfillment of the South as a redemptive community."[6] Kate Chopin's fiction reveals a keen sense of the present and future; she not only understood what was to come but also what had to come. While many of her stories are distinctively within the range of southern storytelling of the late nineteenth century,[7] with such elements as violence, religion, and local color, these narratives extend the tradition into an awareness of the necessity for racial and regional change, the awakening of erotic feelings, relations between the sexes, and the demand for personal liberty. Chopin recognized the distinction of French Louisiana and explored those universal issues which bind it to the world beyond. When we read of these Cane and Mississippi river communities and their varied peoples, we find reflections of the larger self and, indeed, feelings of apocalypse.

Notes

1. *The Complete Works of Kate Chopin*, Vol. 2 (Baton Rouge: Louisiana State University Press, 1969), p. 769. Subsequent references are to this edition and are included parenthetically.
2. "Kate Chopin's Lyrical Short Stories," *Studies in Short Fiction* 11 (Summer 1974): 259.
3. See Per Seyersted, *Kate Chopin: A Critical Biography* (Baton Rouge: Louisiana State University Press, 1969), p. 182.
4. *Selections from Ralph Waldo Emerson*, ed. Stephen E. Whicher (Boston: Houghton Mifflin, 1960), p. 160.
5. See Otis Wheeler, "The Five Awakenings of Edna Pontellier," *Southern Review* 11 (January 1975): 118–128.
6. (Baton Rouge: Louisiana State University Press, 1973), p. 225.
7. See Seyersted, 93–96; Donald A. Ringe, "Cane River World: Kate Chopin's *At Fault* and Related Stores," *Studies in American Fiction* 3 (Autumn 1975): 157–166; and Robert Arner, Special Kate Chopin Issue, *Louisiana Studies* 14 (Spring 1975).